THE AMERICAN BIBLE
CHALLENGE

THE AMERICAN BIBLE
CHALLENGE

A Daily Reader

···· *Volume 1* ····

TROY SCHMIDT

Thomas Nelson
Since 1798

NASHVILLE DALLAS MEXICO CITY RIO DE JANEIRO

Published in Nashville, Tennessee, by Thomas Nelson. Thomas Nelson is a registered trademark of Thomas Nelson, Inc.

Thomas Nelson, Inc., titles may be purchased in bulk for educational, business, fund-raising, or sales promotional use. For information, please e-mail SpecialMarkets@ThomasNelson.com.

Scripture quotations are taken from the Holy Bible, New International Version®, NIV®. Copyright © 1973, 1978, 1984, 2011 by Biblica, Inc.™ Used by permission of Zondervan. All rights reserved worldwide. www.zondervan.com

Library of Congress Control Number: 2013930070

ISBN 978-0-8499-4755-1

Printed in the United States of America

13 14 15 16 17 RRD 6 5 4 3 2 1

To churches and pastors everywhere who
bring the Word of God to people 24/7.

CONTENTS

Week 3

Week 4

Week 5

Week 6

Week 7

Week 8

Week 9

Answers to the Daily Bible Challenges

I first met Troy Schmidt on a soundstage in Los Angeles as we began to cobble together a pilot called *The American Bible Challenge*. While we were both excited about the prospect of such a show, it was tricky ground to walk upon. In fact when I was first approached about hosting the show, my response was, "I don't think so." Not because I was averse to the Bible, but because I was averse to most of the television I had ever seen that was religious in nature. Most of it was too sanitized, and the world I live in is anything but.

I often struggle with the idea of *organized religion*. I love the Lord. In fact my Bible is a kaleidoscope of highlighted passages of text and handwritten comments in the margins. I have been in the same Bible study group for the past fifteen years. We meet on Thursday mornings in the back of a barbecue restaurant, and we have done life together. We have prayed for each other's kids and buried each other's loved ones. It has been the most important "church" I attend. For the past four years I have also led a Bible study for homeless men at the Atlanta Mission in downtown Atlanta. Many have struggled with different forms of addiction but have touched bottom and are making their way back to the surface. They understand the grace of God in a way I have rarely seen. In fact you would pay money just to listen to them pray.

So the challenge for Troy, me, and the rest of the *Bible*

Challenge crew was, how do we make a show about the Bible that proves the teachings within it are still as relevant today as they were thousands of years ago? And also, can we make it fun? (Believe it or not God has a great sense of humor!) What sold me on hosting the show was the decision that the contestants had to give the money away to help someone else.

If you read the Bible, the only people whom Jesus ever had problems with were the religious leaders who had plenty of head knowledge but no heart knowledge. Our contestants have the head knowledge to answer the questions, but more importantly they are putting the scriptures into action. Other people don't have to hear about their faith because that faith is apparent as they live their lives. They reflect Jesus when they just love others.

When Jesus taught, his first recommendation was to repent. I used to think *repent* meant saying, "I'm sorry, I'm sorry, I'm sorry," but it doesn't mean that. It means, "to change the way you think." Someone once said to me that he thought the Bible was a book of rules. I laughed and said, "No, actually it's a love story. In fact the greatest one ever written." The Bible isn't about how bad we have been or how good we try to be. It is about a Creator who made us for his pleasure and paid the price for every shortcoming we could ever have. God is unconditional love in every way possible. We just need to understand that.

My prayer for you as you go through this book is that the Scriptures would fill the dark corners of your life with light. Read up, and let his love pour over you.

> God bless,
> Jeff Foxworthy

INTRODUCTION

When I first heard about *The American Bible Challenge*, I was shocked. "Really? Someone is going to make a game show about the Bible?" This was probably the same reaction most people had. Most television shows satirize Christians. Rarely does any network do anything to uplift and celebrate the Christian faith.

Game Show Network's gamble paid off with millions of loyal Christians gathering the family, watching the show on Thursday nights, and playing the online game. *The American Bible Challenge* quickly became a phenomenon.

I was first approached as a consultant and writer for the show while living in Orlando. My resume in television began with game show research and development, but it was my current position as a campus pastor at First Baptist Church, Windermere, Florida, that caught the producers' attention. A television writer and a pastor? Usually the combination gets a curious raise of the eyebrow. In this case it got me a job.

It was while I worked on the pilot with GSN that they asked me to be the on-camera Bible expert, a role I was not comfortable with. I could see my life inundated with perplexing questions and obscure trivia as I walked into grocery stores or tried to eat meals at restaurants. My whole life would be spent looking like a fool, expected to rattle off David's wives and give the correct order of

Jacob's kids. Thankfully test audiences rejected various aspects of the pilot, one of them my role. That meant I could slip back behind the scenes and enjoy obscurity. Unfortunately much of the pilot flopped, and we had to start at square one. But the commitment of GSN remained strong, bolstered by executives David Schiff, Jean Wiegman, Barry Nugent, and Amy Introcaso-Davis and supported by RelativityREAL's Tom Forman and Odyssey Network's Maura Dunbar.

As we began to retool the show, fresh new faces appeared on the scene and began to breathe new life into *The American Bible Challenge*. Executive producers Janelle Fiorito and Leigh Hampton brought reality and game show experience to the table. Consulting producer Ryan Hopak was a seasoned game show writer and great at comedy. Writer David Dickerson came from the world of greeting cards with an almost encyclopedic mind for the Bible. Rosemarie DiSalvo brought a warmth and sweetness to the room, so missing in our little boy's club. Those six weeks of development and production were hard—but satisfying, now that we've seen the audience appreciation and acceptance of the show.

Much of that success goes to Jeff Foxworthy, a Christian bold enough to step in front of the cameras and say, "Yeah, this is what I believe. So what?" He lets Christians know it's okay to believe in God and laugh! His sincerity and sense of humor have made this show what it is.

The nine-episode television experience of *The American Bible Challenge* prompted this book. I have chosen seven questions from every show, one for each day of the week. There are daily thoughts based on the question's corresponding passage from the Bible, followed by five new questions to challenge you and keep your Bible skills sharp. The answers are in the back, but don't cheat.

I created this book for you to celebrate the number one rated show on GSN that is all about the number one, best-selling book of all time! Maybe you'll do so well answering the questions that someday you can be a contestant on the show.

Troy Schmidt
Windermere, Florida
September 2012
www.troyeschmidt.com

WEEK 1

What Do You *Noah* About the Ark?

Read Genesis 6:9–7:13. • • • •

If God came to you and asked you to do something, what excuse would you give him?

- "I've never done that before."
- "I'm too old (or too young)."
- "But I'm going to face opposition."
- "Oh no, the forecast looks rainy."

When God asks us to do something it's never at a good time. Why? Because it's *his* time, not ours. He sees the big picture. We see only our pictures. God knows the forecasts for centuries to come. We see only the clouds today.

When God asked Noah to build an ark, Noah had plenty of reasons to say no:

- "I've never built an ark before."
- "I'm six hundred years old."
- "The people around me are evil."
- "How am I going to manage a floating zoo?"

Despite the excuses, "Noah did everything just as God commanded him" (Genesis 6:22). If Noah hadn't obeyed, he'd have sunk—literally—and so would we. All of humanity would be drowned in that sea. Thankfully Noah said yes to God's impossible request, and mankind survived.

So what's your reason for saying no to God? Whatever it is, it won't hold water for very long.

TODAY'S BIBLE CHALLENGE

1. What kind of wood was the ark made of?
2. How many decks did the ark have?
3. How many kinds of clean animals did God tell Noah to take?
4. How old was Noah when the floodwaters came on the earth?
5. How many humans were on the ark?

Faithbook—A Friend Request from the Burning Bush

Read Exodus 3. ● ● ● ●

There was no social media in the time of Moses, especially in the wilderness of Midian. There were only sheep and rocks and staffs . . . and bushes. God found a way to reach Moses in the middle of nowhere, where digital reception was less than minimal. Moses' "friend list" was huge, if you count the hundreds of sheep he managed, but none of them ever challenged him or talked to him about deep issues.

Moses wasn't really looking for a friend after forty years doing the same ol' same ol', but God was. God came to Moses because he wanted to involve the shepherd in the greatest, most miraculous event in Old Testament history.

Did God seek Moses? Yes. Did God need Moses? No.

Did Moses seek God? No. Did Moses need God? Yes indeed.

We may not be seeking God, but he is seeking us. We may not want to be friends with God, but he wants to be friends with us. So next time a voice from a burning bush sends you a friend request, listen up. Better yet, listen to the still small voice inside your heart calling out to you. And accept.

TODAY'S BIBLE CHALLENGE

1. Whose flocks was Moses tending when the burning bush appeared?
2. On what mountain did the burning bush appear?
3. What were God's first two words to Moses?
4. What did God ask Moses to remove before he stepped closer to the burning bush?
5. God promised to take the Israelites to a land flowing with what?

In the Name of the Lord of the Rings

Read Exodus 39:1–31. ● ● ● ●

During our Bible readings, it's easy to skip over these sections, these chapters in the Old Testament books, especially Exodus and Leviticus, that describe the tabernacle, the priestly garments, and the dimensions of the utensils for sacrifices. Who cares about that stuff, right? Apparently God does.

When God wanted his people to design a place for worship, he didn't ask them what they wanted to do. Why? Because they would probably have been cheap, more concerned with cost-saving measures than God-worthy quality. The people would have said things such as,

- "Bronze is just as good as gold."
- "Why are we spending so much money on this project?"
- "Who cares about these little details? Let's focus on the big picture."
- "What's an *ephod*, anyway?"

We cut corners because we think it's the wise thing to do, but when it comes to worshiping God, we should never cut corners. God deserves the best we have and all we have, from the biggest picture to the smallest detail. God even cares about the gold rings attached "to the bottom of the shoulders piece on the front of the ephod, close to the seam just above the waistband" (Exodus 39:20). Seem inconsequential? Not to God. He sees every detail, and it all matters to him. To him, that gold ring is precious.

Maybe you should pay attention to the details of your life, too, since they matter so much to God.

TODAY'S BIBLE CHALLENGE

1. How many rows of precious stones were on the priest's breastplate?
2. What did the twelve stones on the breastplate represent?
3. What were the fruits fashioned out of blue, purple, and scarlet yarn and attached to the hem of the robe?
4. What were the noisemakers also attached to the hem of the priest's robe?
5. What was the inscription written on the sacred emblem found on the priest's garment?

Kids Sayeth the Cutest Things—Jonah

Read Jonah 1. ● ● ● ●

God called Jonah to preach a message of repentance to the people of Nineveh, the capital city of the Assyrian Empire, who were, at the time, oppressing the Israelites. It would be like a rabbi in Jerusalem traveling to Iran, walking into downtown Tehran, and saying, "Hey, get your act together, or God is going to destroy you." Probably not the best plan.

So Jonah did what any sensible Israelite would do: he ran and caught a ship going to Tarshish, which was in exactly the opposite direction of Nineveh. When the storm hit the ship, the sailors panicked. That's what sailors are supposed to do. Storms = death. So they looked at all possible reasons why such a thing would happen, and naturally they turned to the spiritual world, wondering which god they needed to satisfy.

And where was Jonah during all this chaos? Asleep. Can you believe it? Even the captain was stunned to find Jonah snoring below deck. Maybe Jonah was tired from running away. Maybe the waves rocked him to sleep. Whatever the reason, God gave him a wake-up call. Thankfully Jonah had caught up on his zzzzz's because for the next three nights, he probably didn't sleep a wink. The fish-belly accommodations were simply horrible.

What about you? Are you asleep? Does God have a plan for you, but you're snoring away? Is there a storm right outside that you're choosing to ignore? You'd better wake up, unless you like the taste of fish. It's better to be going in the direction God called you begrudgingly than to sleep away his will for your life.

TODAY'S BIBLE CHALLENGE

1. In what city did Jonah catch the ship?
2. Whom did each sailor cry out to when the storm hit the ship Jonah had boarded?
3. What did the sailors first throw into the sea to lighten the ship?
4. How did the sailors determine it was Jonah's fault for the storm?
5. What did Jonah suggest the sailors should do to calm the storm?

Swords at the Last Supper Table

Read Luke 22:7–38. • • • •

My mother always told me, "No weapons at the dinner table." She didn't really, because I didn't have any weapons as a kid other than maybe a rubber band or a Boy Scout penknife so dull it couldn't even cut butter.

The Passover meal was one of the most sacred times in the life of a Jew. Once a year all Jews everywhere remembered the night God delivered them from Pharaoh by taking the lives of the firstborn sons in every household not covered by the lamb's blood (Exodus 11–12). Passover was a celebration of God's power, mercy, deliverance, and purpose.

So why would anyone bring swords to the Passover meal? Did they think the lamb would be especially tough this year? Maybe they wanted to provide some entertainment with a round of sword swallowing after the meal? If you were sitting with Jesus Christ—and you understood precisely who he was and what he's capable of doing—would you feel the need to arm yourself? No, because you would know that right in front of you was all the power of the universe. Our tiny swords are no match for the power of Jesus Christ. He just speaks, and people fall down. He can call an army of angels with just a word.

Put away your sword, and rely on the power of God. You might just cut somebody's ear off with that thing.

TODAY'S BIBLE CHALLENGE

1. On what day was the Passover lamb sacrificed?
2. Which two apostles did Jesus send to prepare the Passover feast?
3. What was the man carrying who led the apostles to the house where the Last Supper would occur?
4. Whom did Jesus say Satan wanted to sift like wheat?
5. What was the argument over at the Last Supper?

The Finger of God

Read Exodus 33:12–23. • • • •

I don't have very strong fingers. I used to be able to palm a basketball. I can probably poke an eye out with my index finger, thanks to my extensive research into *The Three Stooges*. My pinkie is useless, except to hit the *a, q, z,* and *p* letters on a keyboard. Balled together, my fingers can gang up and make a fist, but individually they're pretty pitiful.

The Bible personifies God by assigning attributes to him. You can find references to God's eye, arm, ear, nose, hand, mind, even his backside. But let's look at how powerful just his finger is!

- In Exodus 8, the magicians could not reproduce the plague of gnats with their trickery. "This is the finger of God," they cried (8:19).
- In Exodus 31, God wrote the commandments on two stone tablets with his finger.
- In Luke 11, Jesus said he could drive away demons with just his finger.

With just a finger God can create the most incredible miracles and turn an entire nation around. With just a finger God can write the most profound summation of laws that have been replicated in our law books even today. With just a finger God can defeat the world's most persistent enemy.

Do you need the finger of God in your life? You can pick a finger, any finger. It really wouldn't matter as long as it's his.

TODAY'S BIBLE CHALLENGE

1. In Genesis 8, whose sacrifice did God smell as a pleasing aroma that caused him to say he would never again curse the ground?
2. Which two of God's senses notified him to the Israelites' despair in Exodus 2:24–25?
3. When Moses wanted to see God's glory, God told Moses he could not see what part of God's body and live?
4. What part of God's body did he promise would cover Moses when his glory passed by?
5. What part of God's body would he allow Moses to see?

Women of the Bible

Read John 20:1–18. • • • •

The Bible is not a male-dominated *his*tory of *man*kind. Women are just as important as men throughout its pages. It's the women who with endurance and patience, despite public ridicule, gave birth to both Jewish and Christian legacies. Sarah waited four times longer than the average woman to have her first son. Mary faced public scorn for an apparent pregnancy outside of wedlock so she could give birth to the Savior of the world.

Women became political figures and changed the tides of events in the Bible. Esther worked behind the scenes to save her people from annihilation. Deborah was a judge when no man would step up.

God invited women from outside the Israelite family into his. Rahab got her life together and worked for God instead of against his will. Ruth was from the Moabite enemy, but she found herself in the genealogies of David, Solomon, and eventually Jesus Christ.

When Jesus rose from the dead, he chose to appear to the women.

When Paul needed financial support for his ministry trips, he asked women to help.

Thank God he used women in the story of the Bible, and thank God he still uses them in our families to preserve our faith and to show us grace.

What woman has meant the most to you and your relationship with God?

TODAY'S BIBLE CHALLENGE

1. Name the servant of Leah who gave birth to Gad and Asher in Genesis 30.
2. Which prophet raised the son of the Shunammite woman from the dead in 2 Kings 4:8–37?
3. Which Mary spoke to Jesus at the tomb?
4. Who was the dealer of purple cloth who opened her heart to Paul's message in Acts 16?
5. Who was the wife of Aquila who helped Paul spread the gospel in Acts 18?

WEEK 2

My Tweet Lord—Sarah

Read Genesis 18:1–15. • • • •

If she'd had it, Sarah certainly would have used social media to express her emotion when she heard the three mysterious visitors tell her husband, Abraham, that next year she would have a son. Sarah, with her AARP card. Sarah, collecting Social Security. Sarah, old enough to be a great-grandma, giving birth to her first son. Pretty funny? Sarah thought so. In fact she laughed. "Ha! I'm a worn out ol' lady."

The visitor—an angel or some say Jesus himself—said to Abraham, "Why is your wife laughing?" I wonder what kind of a laugh it was. A deep-belly guffaw? A sarcastic chuckle? Either way, Sarah laughed at God. You probably don't want to do that, no matter how ridiculous he may sound.

If you heard God's plan for you right now, what would you do? Scream? Gasp? Maybe cackle? "You want me to do what? I'm going to do that when?" you laugh, with tears in your eyes. Seems hilariously impossible. God has a great sense of humor, right? But he's not joking. If he could allow a grandma to give birth to a healthy child, imagine what he can do with you—at any age. Lead a Bible study of middle schoolers. Go to Peru on a mission trip. Reach inner-city kids with backyard VBS.

Don't laugh—nothing is too hard for the Lord. He can even use . . . you.

TODAY'S BIBLE CHALLENGE

1. Where did the Lord appear to Abraham in Genesis 18?
2. How many men visited Abraham in that location?
3. What did Abraham tell Sarah to make for the visitors?
4. Where was Sarah when she heard the news that she would have a child in one year?
5. What did Sarah deny doing?

The Eye of the Tebow

Read Philippians 4:1–14. ● ● ● ●

"Do not be anxious about anything, but in every situation, by prayer and petition, with thanksgiving, present your requests to God" (Philippians 4:6). Tim Tebow loved to write this verse under his eyes, but it's a verse we should have written in our hearts. Many times we will need to call up this verse and claim it in our situations.

It's hard to imagine quarterbacks living this verse, especially in the extreme situations they face.

- "Do not be anxious about anything"—How about with a three-hundred-pound defensive lineman pouncing at you?
- "But in every situation"—Even when you're down by six and one yard from the end zone with two seconds on the clock in the last quarter?
- "By prayer and petition, with thanksgiving, present your requests to God"—Who has time to talk to God when you're scrambling out of the pocket?

I'm sure Tim Tebow muttered quick prayers in desperate situations, but notice he claimed the verse *before* the kickoff, not during the fourth quarter. He was prepared for the worst situations, setting his heart monitor before things got tough, not trying to remember the verse while his heart rate skyrocketed.

While things are calm, we need to tell ourselves not to worry. We need to present every possible request *now*, so when something comes up we're not surprised. We need to know now that God can handle anything, even if we fumble the ball.

TODAY'S BIBLE CHALLENGE

1. What two women did Paul plead with to reconcile with each other?
2. What does Philippians 4:4 say we should do always?
3. What does Paul say will guard our hearts and minds?
4. What has Paul learned to be in any circumstance?
5. Paul said he could do all things through God who gives him what?

Kids Sayeth the Cutest Things— Moses in the Basket

Read Exodus 2:1–10. • • • •

With the Israelite population getting out of control, the Egyptians decided to exercise post-birth population control by drowning the baby boys in the Nile but allowing the little girls to live. Horrible, right? God didn't like it either. So when Moses' mom could not hide him any longer, she put him in a papyrus basket and sent him down the Nile. The word for this basket in Hebrew is *tebah*, and it's the same word used for "ark," as in Noah's ark.

These two arks are very different. Moses' ark was maybe a yard long. Noah's ark was 150 times longer. Moses' ark was made of reeds from the Nile. Noah's ark was made from cypress wood. One thing they both had in common—they were both covered in pitch or tar to keep them from sinking. And both arks represent the same thing—God's means of saving humanity. Noah's ark saved a righteous family from God's judgment on humanity. Moses' ark saved the man who would lead a nation to safety after God's judgment on Egypt.

Both arks are about salvation, saving those God loves. They were life preservers for everyone on board, leading the world to the ultimate ark, the cross.

The cross is for those today who are sinking in a sea of sin. Hold on—it'll get you through to the other side, where life everlasting awaits you. God always sends an ark to save you from drowning. You just have to climb aboard.

TODAY'S BIBLE CHALLENGE

1. How long did Moses' mom hide him after he was born?
2. What member of Moses' family watched baby Moses float down the Nile?
3. Whom did the attendant of Pharaoh's daughter get to nurse baby Moses?
4. Who named Moses?
5. Why did Pharaoh's daughter say she named her son *Moses*?

CSI Holy Land—Jezebel

Read 1 Kings 21 and 2 Kings 9:30–37. • • • •

The Bible is full of violence. Its pages show the worst in us. That's to be expected. Mankind is prone to hate and kill, but thankfully the bad guys never win.

Jezebel was the baddest bad girl of the Bible. She's so bad, nobody names their little girl Jezebel today. Her name is the female equivalent of Adolf. Jezebel encouraged Baal worship, turning people's hearts away from God. She killed God's prophets. When Elijah killed her prophets, she put out a death warrant on Elijah. When her husband, Ahab, wanted a vineyard, Jezebel had the owner stoned to death because her husband was too weak to take the vineyard himself.

So God had her killed by her own servants. Her own servants couldn't stand her! She was pushed from a high place, splattered on the ground, trampled by horses, and then eaten by dogs so there was nothing left to bury except her skull, feet, and hands. This was her legacy. A horrible death for a horrible person. Someone who once thought herself so important became like dung on the ground.

But this is justice. Jezebel received what she dished out. Jezebel met a fate she deserved. We thank God that he's a God of justice. Hell ultimately is full of Jezebels and Adolfs and whoever else takes pride in murdering the innocent. We wouldn't want it any other way.

TODAY'S BIBLE CHALLENGE

1. According to 1 Kings 18:4, how many prophets did Obadiah hide from Jezebel when she started killing them?
2. Whom did Jezebel have killed for his vineyard?
3. Which prophet said dogs would devour Jezebel by the wall of Jezreel?
4. What did Jezebel put on before her death?
5. What group tossed Jezebel off the tower to her death?

The Beatitudes

Read Matthew 5:1–12. • • • •

According to the original Greek, the word *blessed* found in the Beatitudes means "to be happy." But at first glance, the Beatitudes don't look very happy.

- Poor in spirit
- Mourning
- Meek
- Hungry and thirsty
- Persecuted

This is happiness? According to Jesus it is, because of two reasons.

In Matthew 5:11 Jesus said, "Blessed are you when people insult you, persecute you and falsely say all kinds of evil against you because of me." In other words, if you're doing the things Jesus asked you to do—being a light, following Christ, witnessing to the world—then you are making him happy, even though the world isn't happy with you.

In verse 12, Jesus wrapped it up by saying, "Rejoice and be glad, because great is your reward in heaven, for in the same way they persecuted the prophets who were before you." In other words, don't focus on your situation in the world, an unhappy place, but focus on your eventual home in heaven, a very happy place.

So true Beatitude happiness is found when we make Jesus happy and we focus on the future happy place: his home, heaven. That should make you very, very happy.

TODAY'S BIBLE CHALLENGE

1. According to the Beatitudes, who does Jesus promise will be comforted?
2. What will the meek inherit?
3. Which group will see God?
4. Which group will be called "children of God"?
5. Who did Jesus say was also persecuted?

The Parables

Read Luke 18:1–14. • • • •

You can call a parable a number of things: a juxtaposition, a metaphor, a simile, a story, a proverb, an example, or maybe even a riddle. Whatever you call it, Jesus loved to use them. He didn't spell out exactly what he wanted to say, but he forced his listeners to really listen, to perceive, to examine, to relate these earthly stories into heavenly meanings.

The parables were secrets unlocked by the Holy Spirit. The hard-hearted, without spiritual guidance, could not comprehend the meaning of Jesus' stories. Those open to the Spirit received the meaning and understood. Their hearts were soft, not calloused.

Jesus quoted Isaiah 6:9–10 to explain the benefits of understanding his parables. The hearer will see . . . hear . . . understand . . . and be healed (Matthew 13:14–15). What will be healed? Those hard and calloused hearts. Those difficult and edgy spirits that make us sick. This is true healing: the healing of a heart. So when you read Jesus' parables, ask the Holy Spirit what the meaning is and how it applies to you. Be humble, because you may not like what you hear. Be a doer, and respond by changing your attitude and life. And be healed.

TODAY'S BIBLE CHALLENGE

1. According to the parable of the Good Samaritan in Luke 10, who passed by the wounded man?
2. Jesus told a parable in Luke 11 of a persistent late-night friend who knocks on the door to borrow something. What did he want to borrow?
3. In Luke 16:1–15, what does the manager reduce the first debtor's bill to?
4. In the parables you read for today, who is described as someone who neither feared God nor cared what people thought?
5. In Jesus' parable about the Pharisee and tax collector, the Pharisee is thankful he's not like the tax collector and what three types of men?

Animals of the Bible

Read Genesis 1:20–25. ● ● ● ●

God created the animals—those in the sea, in the air, on the ground—and he saw that they were good. But why did he create them? To give man something to rule over? Maybe. To eat? Looks that way. Companionship? Certainly.

God also created animals so that we could see ourselves in them and understand life a little better:

- The grossness of a dog returning to its vomit is just like a fool going back to his foolish ways (Proverbs 26:11).
- Jesus told his followers to be as shrewd as snakes and as innocent as doves (Matthew 10:16).
- Jesus is described as a lion, an image passed down from his ancestral tribe (Revelation 5:5).
- Peace is like a wolf lying down with a lamb (Isaiah 11:6).

God uses animals to reach and teach us humans. So next time you see that armadillo entering traffic, think about your own hastiness to do things without looking both ways. Or through that arrogant cat who refuses to be petted by its master, maybe you can see your own reluctance to get close to your Master. We can learn a lot about ourselves from the animal kingdom. Just ask your stubborn donkey.

TODAY'S BIBLE CHALLENGE

1. According to Psalm 18, God gave the writer feet that were nimble like what animal?
2. Isaiah 11 says the leopard will lie down with what other animal?
3. What mammal does Daniel 4 tell us that King Nebuchadnezzar began to act like?
4. In Matthew 7, whom does Jesus compare to ferocious wolves in sheep's clothing?
5. Whom did John call the "Lamb of God" in John 1?

WEEK 3

The Parable of the Son Who Moved Back in with His Parents

Read Luke 15:11–32. ● ● ● ●

The lost son in Jesus' parable, who is sometimes known as the prodigal son, is "lost" for three reasons:

1. Arrogance: He didn't listen to advice. He felt he knew best what to do with his time. He didn't want to join his dad's business and decided to make a career out of laziness.
2. Pleasure: He sought after parties instead of purpose. He desired the physical instead of the spiritual. He wanted what felt good now instead of what was best later.
3. Wastefulness: The word *prodigal* means "wasteful," and the son blew all his money on fast living and loose women. He didn't save. He spent.

He returned to his father for one reason: brokenness. The son was at the end of his rope; all his desires had left him penniless. His best friends had all abandoned him. His only friends were a bunch of rude, sloppy pigs.

His father received him back for one reason: grace. The son did nothing to regain his place in the family. Only the father could open the door for his son. Grace, undeserving grace, allowed the son to come home.

It's the story of a lost son, and it's our story too.

If you've left home, come back. God's door is always open for you.

TODAY'S BIBLE CHALLENGE

1. What animal did the younger son grow jealous of because it had food?
2. Who did the younger son realize had it better than him, causing the younger son to return home?
3. What three things did the father put on the son when he arrived home?
4. What did the older son hear as he came in from the fields?
5. What did the older brother accuse his younger brother of squandering their father's money on?

Faithbook—Gideon

Read Judges 7. ● ● ● ●

If you were heading into war with the most feared enemy of the day, would you prefer swords, spears, and armor, or trumpets, jars, and torches? Think carefully. Swords, spears, and armor can kill an oncoming attacker and defend your body from harm. Trumpets, jars, and torches are great for playing jazz while storing up fire. What? The second choice doesn't make any sense.

A musical instrument. A storage vessel. A light in the darkness. For Gideon these three items were the best weapons in the world. Why? Because he had one other weapon: God. Gideon could have come at the enemy with toothpicks, sand, and thimbles, and somehow God would have found a way to win. Gideon believed the trumpet would proclaim God's victory. He had the faith to fill thousands of jars. And he knew that God wanted to bring a light into the enemy territory.

What weapons do you need to bring to your battle—yours or God's?

TODAY'S BIBLE CHALLENGE

1. What was Gideon's other name?
2. When Gideon told his army that any man who was afraid to attack the Midianites could go home, how many left?
3. How many men brought the water to their mouths when drinking from the river, qualifying them to fight in Gideon's army?
4. Gideon heard a dream from a man who encouraged him to attack the Midianites. What tumbled down in this man's dream and crushed the Midianite tent?
5. Name the two Midianite leaders Gideon captured.

Genesis or Genesis

Read Genesis 15. ● ● ● ●

Genesis has some memorable lines:

- In the beginning God created the heavens and the earth. (1:1)
- Then God said, "Let us make mankind in our image . . ." (1:26)
- Am I my brother's keeper? (4:9)
- God himself will provide the lamb for the burnt offering, my son. (22:8)
- So then, it was not you who sent me here, but God. (45:8)

But probably the one verse that has the most profound impact is Genesis 15:6: "Abram believed the LORD, and he credited it to him as righteousness." This statement isn't as catchy as the others, but it helps us to understand how someone truly believes in God. Abram knew of God; he talked to him all the time. Abram knew the history of God and his characteristics. Abram knew everything he could, but he didn't believe God until he trusted him.

When the Lord said to Abram, "Look up at the sky and count the stars—if indeed you can count them. . . . So shall your offspring be" (15:5), Abram could have filed that into his brain under Promises or Quotes from God. But instead he filed it in his heart, under Relationships. We trust people with whom we have a relationship. We love them. Not only do we know their qualities and information about them, but we believe in them because we trust them.

Genesis 15:6 defined *belief* for the entire Bible. It's the same kind of belief needed for a relationship with Jesus. Love, trust . . . and believe.

TODAY'S BIBLE CHALLENGE

1. If Abram didn't have a son, who could have inherited his estate?
2. What did the Lord tell Abram to look up and count?
3. What five animals did the Lord ask Abram to bring to him as a sacrifice for the covenant?
4. What came down and tried to eat the animal carcasses?
5. The Lord foretold that the Israelites would be strangers in a country for how many years?

Kids Sayeth the Cutest Things—David and Goliath

Read 1 Samuel 17:40–58. • • • •

Maybe you've heard the expression, "Hurt people hurt people." Those who have been criticized or rejected criticize and reject others to make themselves feel bigger. Goliath needed some serious counseling. As a kid, Goliath must have been called *string bean* on the playground. He most likely was a klutz, his enormous body taking years to develop its coordination. The girls probably rejected any advances from this gangly boy, a freakish gargantuan in their eyes.

Then Goliath became a giant. The taunting stopped. His body became agile and deadly. The girls succumbed to Goliath's desires more likely out of fear than love. Goliath turned to a Philistine god that made him feel better about himself and didn't make him feel guilty for all the abuse he handed back to the world. Now it was Goliath's turn to show the world who was boss.

David stepped into the Valley of Elah, and the first thing Goliath noticed was David's young, glowing, healthy, and handsome good looks—and the verse says Goliath despised him (v. 42). David was everything Goliath never was. It wasn't the army David represented or even the God David stood up for that offended Goliath. Goliath, the most threatening force on the battlefield, may have simply been jealous of this dashing young lad who had everything Goliath wanted but never had.

We must be careful not to become Goliaths in our world, hurting those around us because we're jealous of what they have. Our hatred could cause us to lose our heads.

TODAY'S BIBLE CHALLENGE

1. Besides the stones, shepherd's bag, and sling, what did David take to the fight against the Philistine?
2. What three weapons did David say the Philistine was armed with?
3. Whose sword did David use to cut off the Philistine's head?
4. Where did David take the Philistine's head?
5. Where did David put the Philistine's weapons?

Genealogy of Jesus

Read Matthew 1:1–17. ● ● ● ●

I don't know if I would publicize my genealogy if it looked like Jesus':

- Two men who had sex with their wives' handmaidens
- One who slept with his daughter-in-law
- A prostitute
- Someone who killed the husband of a woman he'd gotten pregnant
- A line of political leaders who split and destroyed Israel

Sure, there are some highlights in there, but the lowlifes overshadow the good.

If Jesus, God himself who knits and forms humanity in the womb, could design any family line he wanted, why choose this one? Because if he came through a perfect line of godly people, it would send a message that we needed to be bred perfectly to be included in God's spiritual family. We would think any rotten branch on our family tree immediately disqualified us from righteousness. "Sorry, your dad was a train robber. You're out!" By coming through a line of imperfect people, Jesus shows us that he has risen above his heritage. Just because he came from sinners doesn't mean he had to be a sinner.

Our parents may have been alcoholics or absentees. Or maybe our grandparents' faces showed up routinely on the post office "Wanted" posters. Your great-great grandparents could have marched with Stalin. It doesn't mean you have to be like them. Jesus proved that to be true. A believer enters a new family line—the adopted sons and daughters of God the Father. That's a family tree you should be happy to share.

TODAY'S BIBLE CHALLENGE

1. Matthew's genealogy of Jesus begins with what person?
2. Matthew's genealogy of Jesus contains what woman who tricked her father-in-law into sleeping with her in Genesis 38?
3. According to Matthew, who was the son of Boaz and Ruth?
4. Who is the father of Joseph, the husband of Mary?
5. Three sets of how many generations are mentioned in Matthew's genealogy?

It's Time

Read Ecclesiastes 3:1–8. • • • •

Solomon makes a profound statement in Ecclesiastes 3. So profound, the Byrds recorded a song using some of his lyrics called, "Turn, Turn, Turn."

Everything listed in verses 2–8 is a polar contrast to the adjacent word. Be born and die. Plant and uproot. Kill and heal. Tear down and build up. Life is lived in and between the extremes. Using these well-defined boundaries, Solomon expresses that anything *can* happen in this world. The best and the worst. The good and the bad. Sin causes an unpredictable world where we strive to pull our lives away from God's purpose and sometimes succeed.

Solomon is also saying that everything *will* happen. We will all be born, and we will all die. There's nothing we can do about it. People will weep, and people will laugh. We can't be shocked by the tearing of relationships, nor can we always expect that everything will mend. At some point in our lives, all of us will experience scattering and gathering, searching and giving up, loving and hating. Be prepared.

Solomon also says that life naturally changes like the seasons. You can't stop winter from coming, just as war is inevitable in some parts of the world. Then again spring comes, too, and the world eventually discovers peace. These changes aren't always our fault, and we don't have to blame ourselves for winter. We just have to accept it.

It is cliché to say, "Hey, that's life," but Solomon poetically puts it in such a way that we have to agree. Life ebbs and flows like the ocean, and you just have to ride the waves.

TODAY'S BIBLE CHALLENGE

1. According to Ecclesiastes 3, there's a time to be born and a time to what?
2. There's a time to kill and a time to what?
3. There's a time to weep and a time to what?
4. There's a time to search and a time to what?
5. There's a time to love and a time to what?

Proverbs

Read Proverbs 1. • • • •

Proverbs is a collection of wisdom from Solomon as well as other wise men from the Bible. It's written from the perspective of a teacher talking to his pupil, offering advice on how to have an impact on the next generation. It's a book about choice and voice. Which voice are we going to choose to listen to?

- The voice of wisdom expresses itself out in the open, in the streets. She has nothing to hide. Wisdom cries out for followers. She thinks of the future and the impact of our choices today on our lives tomorrow. She looks out for our safety. Wisdom sees both sides and knows the schemes of her opponent.
- The voice of foolishness whispers in the shadows and back rooms. She seeks self-satisfaction for the moment. The future is not important, only the needs of now. Foolishness does not think or process the ramifications of choice. She wants what she does not have. She risks everything to feel pleasure.

Who has your ear? Who are you listening to? Don't end up like the wise writer of the wisest book of the Bible who listened to the wrong voices and made choices that destroyed his kingdom.

Even his son did not listen to Solomon's commands because he didn't see his father following them in his personal life. Even the wise can end up fools.

TODAY'S BIBLE CHALLENGE

1. According to Proverbs 1, what is the beginning of knowledge?
2. What two people should a son listen to?
3. Who cries aloud from the public square in Proverbs 1?
4. According to Proverbs 2, whose house leads to death?
5. In Proverbs 3, if you honor the Lord with your wealth, what will happen to your barns?

WEEK 4

Jesus Picked Up the Tab

Read John 13. ● ● ● ●

Jesus organized his disciples into the Upper Room for Passover, then began to wash their feet. That's gross, especially when you think about a first-century sandaled foot in dusty ol' Jerusalem during the busy Passover celebration. Foot washing was the most humbling job a person could do to serve the lowest part of another person's body.

Why did he do it? According to Luke 22, the disciples had been arguing about who would be greatest. Did Jesus listen and shake his head? Roll his eyes? Heave a deep sigh then drop his chin to his chest? Maybe, but Jesus also turned it into a teachable moment and pulled out the towel and wash basin. Jesus said, "You call me 'Teacher' and 'Lord,' and rightly so, for that is what I am. Now that I, your Lord and Teacher, have washed your feet, you also should wash one another's feet" (John 13:13–14). Here's greatness. The greatest one is the one who serves.

Can you imagine having an argument about greatness after Jesus washed your feet? Before I judge the disciples' arrogance, I must not forget how I put my "great" schedule and my "great" plans before God's. There are many times I put my "great" needs ahead of others and refuse to serve them. I'm not sitting at the table with Jesus, but I'm just as guilty of elevating my greatness above Christ. And yet, Jesus probably just sighs at me and asks, "When is he going to learn?"

TODAY'S BIBLE CHALLENGE

1. What did Jesus wrap around his waist before washing the disciples' feet?
2. Besides his feet, what did Simon Peter say needed to be washed?
3. What did Jesus hand to Judas to indicate he was Jesus' betrayer?
4. Who was in charge of the disciples' money?
5. Jesus predicted Peter would deny him three times before what bird crowed?

Biblical Greeting Cards—Lot

Read Genesis 19. • • • •

Before the destruction of Sodom and Gomorrah, the two men (who were angels) pleaded with Lot and his family to get out of town. The men told Lot not to look back at the city's destruction because anyone who did would turn to salt.

That's a tough request. Wouldn't you want to see such cool explosions, like out of a science-fiction movie? How could you not look back?

Lot's wife did.

Looking back does two things—it slows down your escape, and it takes you back down memory lane. God was worried about their safety and didn't want them to get caught in the fire-and-brimstone storm. He also didn't want them longing for the good ol' days.

For the first time in Genesis, we read that Lot had a family, which would lead us to believe that his wife was from Sodom or Gomorrah. This probably explains why she looked back. Suddenly she felt sorry for her sexually corrupt hometown. God didn't want her longing for Sodom. He wanted her to leave it behind and look ahead to the future. By turning to salt, she returned to the ground, literally going the way of the earth. Her thoughts became dirt, and her memories blew away like dust in the wind.

Don't yearn for the sinful days of your past. Look forward to a sinless future in heaven with your Savior.

TODAY'S BIBLE CHALLENGE

1. The Lord destroyed Sodom and Gomorrah before Lot reached what city?
2. What did the Lord rain down on Sodom and Gomorrah?
3. Which two of Lot's family members refused to leave town?
4. Whom did Lot's older daughter give birth to?
5. Whom did Lot's younger daughter give birth to?

Set Phasers to Bless—Zadok

Read 1 Kings 1:32–40. • • • •

Zadok is one of those names from the Bible that makes you ask, "Who? Never heard of this guy." Well, if you were King David, then you knew him quite well. Zadok was a priest during his reign. Zadok helped to transport the ark. He loyally stayed by David's side, working with Nathan, the famous prophet. The Zadokites (descendants of Zadok) remained loyal as priests even when the Levites strayed.

So you still don't know the name? What does it matter? God knew the name and rewarded Zadok for his faithfulness. David knew the name and considered him loyal. Solomon knew the name and called him Israel's priest. There are names in the Bible that are obscure to us but were vitally important to God's history.

What about you? Are you a famous celebrity in the world of Christianity, or a humble servant in a small country church in Mississippi? Who cares? Nothing else matters except God knowing your name.

TODAY'S BIBLE CHALLENGE

1. In 2 Samuel 15, what did Zadok carry into Jerusalem with the Levites?
2. Where did David command that the next king be anointed?
3. Which son of David did Zadok anoint as king?
4. Which son of Zadok helped to deliver the news that Absalom was dead in 2 Samuel 18?
5. Which major prophet mentions Zadok's priestly line in his story of the temple restoration?

Lyrical Miracles—Amazing Grace

Read Ephesians 2. ● ● ● ●

Is grace really that amazing?

> If it wasn't for grace, we'd be dead in our sins.
>> If it wasn't for grace, we would deserve God's wrath.
> Because of grace, we are alive now.
>> Because of grace, we have been saved.
> Through grace, God has shown his kindness to us.
>> Through grace, God has given us a gift.
> Thanks to grace, I don't have to work to save myself.
>> Thanks to grace, I have a purpose to do good works.
> Amazing grace? Still is. Always will be.

TODAY'S BIBLE CHALLENGE

1. According to Ephesians 2, God made us alive in Christ even when we were dead in what?
2. Since we are saved by grace and not by works, what can we not do?
3. We were created in Christ Jesus to do what?
4. What has brought those "who once were far away" near?
5. What did Christ preach to those far away and near?

Languages at Pentecost

Read Acts 2:1–21. ● ● ● ●

Peter preached the first sermon on Pentecost, and the place went wild. Tongues of fire appeared over the audience's heads, and everyone began to speak in other languages. Amazed by the miracle, the people asked, "What does this mean?" (Acts 2:12). Good question. The answer: passion and purpose.

Ever heard the expression, "He was on fire for the Lord"? At Pentecost the people, filled with the Holy Spirit, were spiritually "set on fire." It's the perfect metaphor. Fires spread, igniting anything around them, until they build into burning blazes.

God wanted to use Peter's audience to set the world passionately on fire with the message of the gospel. The languages gave them direction and a purpose—to take that fire into the whole world, beyond Israel, crossing borders to places they would never normally go and to people whose languages they may not speak. The miracle expressed an urgency in their task—fires are impatient and thorough; they burn up everything in their paths; they don't wait around. The fire ignited that day blazed all over the world for thousands of years to you and me. Now we must carry that torch to all nations.

Are you on fire? Then speak up!

TODAY'S BIBLE CHALLENGE

1. What did the arrival of the Holy Spirit sound like at Pentecost?
2. What kind of structure were the believers in when the Holy Spirit arrived at Pentecost?
3. What region did the crowd know the tongue-speakers were originally from?
4. What did the crowd think the tongue-speakers had too much of?
5. When Peter addressed the crowd after this incident, who was the first Old Testament prophet he quoted?

Small but Wise

Read Proverbs 30. ● ● ● ●

People go to college, get their degrees, move on to graduate school, then eventually get their doctorates; but sometimes they're dumber than ants. Agur, the author of this proverb, stated that the small things of the earth, things you could crush under your foot, can teach you a thing or two no matter how many degrees hang on your wall.

- Ants have very little strength, but they store up their food in the summer. Being strong doesn't mean you're wise. Being weak doesn't mean you're stupid.
- Ants don't say, "I've had a busy season, and I need a break." They work hard to get the important tasks done when they need to get done.
- Ants don't go hungry when the winter hits, because they've worked all summer to stock their shelves. Rest in the winter, they say, when there's no place to go and we're trapped inside. Work in the summer, when the food supplies are plentiful.
- Ants see the big picture, following the plan and never deviating from the purpose.

So before you go outside and take your next step, be careful not to crush that ant. He might as well have graduated from Harvard.

TODAY'S BIBLE CHALLENGE

1. In Proverbs 30, what do the leech's two daughters cry?
2. What makes the ants so wise?
3. The small but wise hyraxes make their homes in what?
4. The locusts are small yet wise because they advance in ranks without what?
5. The lizard is wise because it's easily captured and yet it can be found where?

Peter, Paul, and Mary

Read Luke 1:26–56. • • • •

In the 1960s Peter, Paul, and Mary were a popular folk group, but the legacy of the original Peter, Paul, and Mary started two thousand years ago and will continue for an eternity to come.

- Mary was the first of the three to say yes to God's will and allowed the Savior of humanity to be born through her. Mary persevered through public scorn because of this mysterious pregnancy to accomplish what God asked her to do.
- Peter was the first to preach a fiery sermon and led the first revival in church history. He slipped in and out of prison and had the scars on his back to prove it.
- Paul was the first missionary to take the gospel message to the entire world, crossing borders and starting churches all over the map. His dramatic conversion stunned the religious world and, undeterred, Paul boasted of his suffering.

Only one book of the Bible mentions all three of them—Acts. And it was their "acts" that made all the difference.

These three people said yes to God's will for their lives and paid the price. And aren't we glad they did? We won't be singing

"Puff the Magic Dragon" into eternity, but we will be singing praises to God because of what Peter, Paul, and Mary did.

TODAY'S BIBLE CHALLENGE

1. About how many new believers were added after Peter's speech on Pentecost?
2. How long did Mary stay with Elizabeth for her visit?
3. What is the last book of the Bible where Mary the mother of Jesus is mentioned?
4. What city does Acts 9 tell us Paul was from?
5. What did Saul do immediately after his sight was restored?

WEEK 5

My Tweet Lord—Barabbas

Read Matthew 27:15–26. • • • •

Can you imagine Barabbas running out of the prison cell, updating his Twitter status, screaming, "I'm free! I'm free!"? Barabbas, a convicted murderer and political insurrectionist whom Matthew describes as "a well-known prisoner" (27:16), was released from incarceration because of public opinion. Barabbas frequented the jail cell, so he was probably on a first-name basis with the guards. How did Barabbas get set free? Jesus. Jesus took his place in the jail. Barabbas, a guilty man, was let go and replaced by a totally innocent man.

You wonder how Barabbas felt just hours later if he saw Jesus on the cross, thinking, *That could have been me.* How do you feel as you think of Jesus, who stepped in and died for you and your sins? Are you humbled? Relieved? Are you so happy that you want to proclaim from your social media, "I'm free! I'm free! Jesus has set me free!"?

TODAY'S BIBLE CHALLENGE

1. What was Barabbas's full name?
2. What Roman leader let Barabbas go?
3. Who had a dream about Jesus that haunted her all the next day?
4. When asked what crime Jesus had committed, what was the crowd's response?
5. Who took credit for Jesus' death when Pilate declared himself innocent of it?

Lyrical Miracles—Zacchaeus

Read Luke 19:1–10. • • • •

"Zacchaeus was a wee little man," as the famous song about him goes. But with Zacchaeus's powerful status as tax collector, nobody would dare walk up to him and call him that.

"Hey, wee little Zacchaeus-man! What do I owe on my 1040?"

His response: "More taxes for you!"

Nobody liked the tax collectors, who could charge outrageous rates based on whim. No government regulations for this job. These guys were corrupt and hated by their communities.

Even this short little corrupt guy got a chance to meet someone who changed his life. Zacchaeus, lost in the crowd, was found by Jesus, who asked to spend some time with him—a man nobody wanted to spend any time with at all.

It doesn't matter how tall you are. It doesn't matter how sinful you are, what your job is, or what others think of you—Jesus wants to stop by your house with all his love, his grace, and his acceptance. Would you let him in? Zacchaeus did.

TODAY'S BIBLE CHALLENGE

1. In what town was Zacchaeus living?
2. What was Zacchaeus's job?
3. What kind of a tree did Zacchaeus climb to see Jesus?
4. After meeting Jesus, Zacchaeus promised to pay back those he had cheated how many times the amount he had stolen?
5. As a result of Zacchaeus's actions, what did Jesus claim had come to Zacchaeus's house that day?

Biblical Classified Ads— Aaron's Staff

Read Numbers 17. ● ● ● ●

God asked Moses to collect staffs from the Twelve Tribes. The next day they woke up and found Aaron's staff had not only budded but blossomed and produced almonds. A dead stick came to life and produced fruit. This miracle stopped the grumbling of the Israelites, who immediately recognized the power of God. The staff was so legendary, it received a place inside the ark next to the tablets containing the Ten Commandments and the jar of manna (Hebrews 9:4).

Why was it such a big deal? The staff represented the tribe of Levi, setting them aside for the role of priests. But it also showed the Israelites—and us—that God can take deadwood and bring it to life—budding, blossoming, and producing fruit.

It was a miracle that God could do with an old stick. It's still a miracle he does with us. So if you feel like you're deadwood or an old stick in the mud, don't worry. God can make you blossom again.

TODAY'S BIBLE CHALLENGE

1. What did Aaron's staff turn into when he threw it before the Pharaoh in Exodus 10?
2. Which three plagues of Exodus 7 and 8 happened as a direct result of Aaron's staff?
3. From which person in each tribe were the staffs collected in Numbers 17?
4. What was written on each staff?
5. What did they place the staffs in front of?

Smote by an Angel—Herod

Read Acts 12. • • • •

I like to listen to athletes or singers after they've won an award. I always hope they'll start off by saying, "I'd like to thank God for this honor." Inside my heart, I'm fist-pumping. "Yes! God gets the glory!"

Herod Agrippa was born into the line of corrupt kings, which included Herod the Great, who murdered babies in order to find Jesus. God didn't like the Herod family, and the feeling was mutual. Herod Agrippa in Acts 12 pushed God too far while addressing a crowd. It says he spoke in such a way that the people responded, "This guy is a god!" Whether it was his public speaking skills, his charisma, or his dashing good looks, Herod didn't give God the credit for his speech. Instead, he responded, "I'd like to thank myself for this award!"

God sent an angel who delivered a nasty worm to Herod's guts, and it ate him from the inside out. Our selfishness does exactly that. It eats us up from the inside. Our pride brings us to early deaths. We don't have to wait to get buried in the ground to get eaten by worms. Our deaths begin the moment we take credit for our lives and forget to mention God. It's called selfishness.

So who would you like to thank for what you've achieved in this life? Be careful.

TODAY'S BIBLE CHALLENGE

1. Whom did Peter say the Lord sent to rescue him from Herod's clutches?
2. After Peter's escape from prison, whom did Herod have executed?
3. Whom had Herod been quarreling with before he made his speech?
4. What did Herod put on before he made his speech?
5. Herod died, but what happened next to the word of God?

False Gods

Read 1 Kings 11:1–13. • • • •

False gods come in all shapes and sizes. Some tempt you to commit sexual perversions; others ask you to incinerate your children in fire. What was the appeal of these gods, and how did they manage to be a thorn in the side of Israel for so long? Were the people stupid or ignorant?

Stupidity or wisdom had nothing to do with it. Solomon, the wisest king who ever lived, fell into the temptation trap of false gods. How did he stumble? Relationships. Solomon developed a tangled web of wives and concubines that confused his focus on what was important. He got so wrapped up in the world that he allowed the world to wrap itself around him. Solomon didn't just wink at the pagan worship; he approved it. He had temples built for these gods. This is the same Solomon who heard directly from God, who built a magnificent temple in Jerusalem, who was the son of David!

We must be careful of the relationships we allow to influence our lives. They could lead us to do something very stupid. Just ask Solomon.

TODAY'S BIBLE CHALLENGE

1. In Deuteronomy 7, God wanted to tear down the poles of what goddess?
2. Which god's statue was found face down with its hands and head broken off in 1 Samuel 5?
3. Who is the detestable god of the Moabites?
4. Who is the detestable god of the Ammonites?
5. In Acts 19, which goddess did the silversmith Demetrius build silver shrines for?

I Am

Read John 10:7–21. ● ● ● ●

The most definitive "I am" statement comes from God speaking to Moses through the burning bush. Moses asked, "Who do I say told me to do these things? What's your name?"

God said to Moses, "I AM WHO I AM" (Exodus 3:14). No noun or adjective followed that "I am" statement. I would say, "I am an American," or "I am tall." I use a description to differentiate myself from others. God defines himself with himself. It's the simplest and purest form of explanation: "I am me," God says. "There is no other."

Jesus used "I am" statements in many forms to connect his audiences to what God said in Exodus, communicating to everyone that he was God. Jesus' self-identification drove people crazy. They understood what he was saying, and they didn't like it. Jesus said, "Look, this is who I am, like it or not. Will you accept it?"

God cannot change who he is, but if you accept who he is, then he can change who you are and who you will become. Accept the I AM, and don't try to change who *he is*.

TODAY'S BIBLE CHALLENGE

1. What miracle in John 6 prompted Jesus to say, "I am the bread of life"?
2. In John 6, with what Old Testament hero does Jesus contrast himself?
3. In reference to what animal does Jesus say, "I am the gate"?
4. Jesus said, "I am the good shepherd," unlike the hired hand who runs from what animal?
5. The death of what friend caused Jesus to say, "I am the resurrection and the life" in John 11?

Daniel

Read Daniel 1. ● ● ● ●

What separates Daniel from Adam, Abraham, Jacob, Moses, David, and Solomon? Mainly that you don't hear anything bad about him. Daniel is always portrayed positively:

- He stayed true to his faith, never wavering despite public opinion.
- He hung out with guys who shared his conviction.
- He remained a servant to God despite his climb up the political ladder.
- He represented a true believer while his country floundered because of their lack of faith.
- He was used by God to receive a very interesting vision that probably nobody but Daniel understands to this day.

Was Daniel perfect? No way. Only Jesus was perfect. But Daniel's good outweighed his bad. His bad was so insignificant that it was never worth mentioning.

Wouldn't you want your story to be written like Daniel's? Nothing but positive reviews.

TODAY'S BIBLE CHALLENGE

1. What did Nebuchadnezzar take to the temple of his god in Babylonia and put in the treasure house?
2. How many years were the young Israelite men trained in Babylonian culture?
3. What were the Jewish names of Daniel's three friends?
4. What was Daniel's Babylonian name?
5. Daniel remained in exile until the first year of what king?

WEEK 6

Man Has Fallen and He Can't Get Up

Read Genesis 3. • • • •

The word *fall* never appears in the Genesis 3 account of Adam and Eve disobeying God's command, but the word works so well in context.

- Falling is stumbling out of control in a direction the person doesn't want to go.
- A person who is falling was once in a higher position and quickly descends to a lower position.
- Pain usually follows the falling as the person hits the bottom.
- In seasonal talk, fall is followed by winter, symbolically a time of death.

When humanity *fell* in the garden of Eden, these images all describe what happened as a result of disobedience.

- Sin caused man to stumble away from God, resulting in separation.
- Man once was in a close relationship, but sin caused him to descend into a distant relationship.

- The pain of this separation was felt physically, emotionally, and spiritually as man hit rock bottom.
- From the fall of man, death resulted.

When man *fell* in the garden, he couldn't get up . . . on his own. Only the One he fell from could restore his position. God helped us get back up on our feet through the love and sacrifice of Jesus Christ.

TODAY'S BIBLE CHALLENGE

1. Where was the tree located that God told Eve not to eat from?
2. What happened to Adam's and Eve's eyes when they ate the fruit?
3. What kind of leaves did Adam and Eve sew together after they sinned?
4. When did the Lord God walk through the garden?
5. Because of the garden deception, what two botanical nuisances cursed the ground?

Mad Verses—Proverbs 3:5–6

Read Proverbs 3. ● ● ● ●

How do you trust God? According to Proverbs 3:5–6,

- I must trust *only one thing* in my life and nothing more—God. This means I cannot trust any person or thing on this earth other than him. He gets my sole trust.
- I must trust God *with all my heart*. The heart is the center of relationship, not an emotional connection, but the core of our convictions. We trust out of love.
- I must trust God and *not lean on my own* understanding, because once my brain gets involved and tries to figure it out—the why, how, when, and who—I get all confused. I must trust God's understanding of me and not trust myself.
- I must trust God and *submit to him*, putting him in charge and keeping my hands out of my own business.
- As I trust I *walk down the straight paths* he has created.

Trust only God. Trust him out of love. Trust him even if you can't understand it. Trust him as you walk in his paths.

TODAY'S BIBLE CHALLENGE

1. According to Proverbs 3, if the son does not forget the father's teaching, what will be prolonged?
2. If we are not wise in our own eyes, what will be nourished?
3. If we honor the Lord with our wealth, what will be filled to overflowing?
4. What did the Lord use to lay the earth's foundation?
5. Whom should we not tell to come back tomorrow if we already have what they want from us?

Love Lines—Song of Songs

Read Song of Songs 1. ● ● ● ●

It's probably the only book of the Bible that makes you blush. It feels so . . . out of place. Most pastors refuse to preach out of it, especially during family hour. Maybe there will be a special Wednesday night study of Solomon's love song for couples, behind closed doors with police tape over the door reading, "Keep out!"

But the Song of Songs is one of sixty-six books of the Bible that prudent and righteous people for over two thousand years have approved and listed as important enough to make the cut. Why? It's not a story of X-rated lust but of passion. We cannot deny that we've been designed with a desire for a person of the opposite sex. Where did that emotional response come from? Song of Songs tells us that God encourages that kind of love within the confines of a committed marriage.

So don't shy away from Solomon's most intimate writings. If you're single, find a godly person who sets your soul on fire and get married. If you're married, keep that fire blazing with lessons learned from the poetical pages of this passionate book.

TODAY'S BIBLE CHALLENGE

1. The woman says the man's love is more delightful than what beverage?
2. The woman calls herself dark like the tents of what place?
3. Why does the woman believe people are staring at her?
4. What kind of jewelry does the man promise to make the woman?
5. To what birds does he compare her eyes?

CSI Holy Land—Joseph

Read Genesis 37. • • • •

If I were Joseph, I would be pretty upset. His brothers, out of jealousy over a stupid colorful coat, pushed him into a cistern and then sold him off to traders who carted him off to Egypt, where he got thrown in jail and forgotten for years. Joseph, a seventeen-year-old at the prime of his life, outnumbered and overwhelmed, blamed for things he didn't do, uprooted and transplanted to a place he didn't want to go, was abandoned. Wouldn't you be upset?

Joseph probably was, at some point, but he saw the good in it. Later, as God blessed him and placed him into the second-highest position in the most powerful nation on earth, Joseph met up with his brothers again. After testing and toying with them, Joseph revealed his identity. He said, "You intended to harm me, but God intended it for good to accomplish what is now being done, the saving of many lives" (Genesis 50:20).

Wow. Joseph is a better man than I am. I would see what I had lost. Joseph saw what he had gained. I would see my missed opportunities. Joseph saw God's opportunities. I would see the death of me. Joseph saw the saved lives of many people. No wonder his brothers hated him. He was a better man than all of them.

TODAY'S BIBLE CHALLENGE

1. How old was Joseph when he first tattled on his brothers?
2. Joseph's first dream involved sheaves of what?
3. Joseph's second dream involved what three objects in space?
4. Which brother first defended Joseph and kept the brothers from killing him?
5. Which brother suggested selling him to the traders?

Feeding the Five Thousand

Read Mark 6:30–44. ● ● ● ●

As he watched his five-thousand-member audience, Jesus saw a need—hunger—and decided to fulfill that need by feeding the large crowd with an abundance of bread and fish that came out of nowhere.

Every gospel account of the story says that everyone who ate that day was satisfied. Sounds of "I'm full" or "I couldn't eat another bite" were heard throughout the outdoor café. People leaned back and patted their stomachs as they picked their teeth. And there were leftovers—baskets and baskets of leftovers. Jesus stuffed everyone full and beyond fulfillment. So full, nobody could imagine taking any of it home.

This miracle shows the heart of God. God doesn't ask us to take a bite of fish and pass it to the next person. He doesn't show us the bread then slap our hands when we reach for it. God fills our plates so high, we can't possibly eat everything on them.

As we look to the blessings in our lives, we should never say that God has given us only a taste of his love. We should always be able to say that God has overwhelmed us to satisfaction with his grace. His love overflows our cups and spills onto our laps. So enjoy the smorgasbord of God's blessings. And don't worry, he'll make more.

TODAY'S BIBLE CHALLENGE

1. How much money did the disciples calculate it would cost to feed the five thousand?
2. How many loaves did the disciples find before feeding the five thousand?
3. How many fish did the disciples find before feeding the five thousand?
4. Jesus directed the people to sit in groups of how many?
5. Who were the five thousand, men or women?

One Hundred Fifty Years Old

Read Genesis 5. ● ● ● ●

Genesis 5 contains the genealogies of the people who lived before the Flood. They were unfathomably old, most of them living between seven hundred and nine hundred years. That's more than six hundred years carrying an AARP card. Our Social Security system would be totally bankrupt, unless the retirement age was changed to eight hundred years old.

Can you imagine nine hundred years of living on this earth? I can't. It doesn't seem appealing at all. Especially not with what's waiting for all believers on the other side of life. The fact that some people lived to one hundred fifty after the Flood shouldn't surprise us. Some believe the Bible is inaccurate because it portrays such outrageous ages. If you consider their diet, the atmosphere, the lack of diseases that hadn't yet mutated, no cars, few wars, and few people, it's not so crazy.

But don't forget this—God wanted people like Moses and Joshua to live a long time. He had a lot to do through them. He had purposes for them, and it took more than one hundred years to accomplish them. If God wants you to live, you ain't gonna die!

We shouldn't be concerned with how many years we are going to live. We should be concerned with how we're going to live all those years. We should make sure every year is filled with God's purpose and not our own desires. Make every day, week, month, and year count; and let God determine when it's time to call it quits.

TODAY'S BIBLE CHALLENGE

1. In Genesis 5, who is the only son of Adam and Eve mentioned?
2. Whom did Seth father?
3. Who lived longest: Adam, Seth, or Enosh?
4. Whom in Genesis did God take away?
5. Who was Noah's father?

The Resurrection

Read 1 Corinthians 15. • • • •

What would life be like without the resurrection?

- We would have a dead prophet—a good man—lying cold in a stone tomb. "He had so much potential," his followers would say. "He really made us feel good about ourselves."
- Funerals today would be filled with a different kind of hope: "We hope the dearly departed is with God and sadly we don't know for sure."
- Good Friday would be Just Another Friday, no different than another day. Hard to believe we'd celebrate the Death of Jesus Day.
- There would be no Easter. We'd still be celebrating Passover, heralding Moses' deliverance of the Jews through the parted Red Sea as the greatest miracle of all time.
- Forget Christmas. The birth of another prophet would make no difference. We don't celebrate Elijah's birth or Isaiah's.
- We would go through life fearing death. It would be like going to the airport without any luggage and getting on a flight with no idea where it was taking you for the rest

of eternity. Some place hot and miserable? Or maybe it'll be pleasant. We'd have no assurance. Who would look forward to that? What would you take with you?

The resurrection changes the way we celebrate life and anticipate death with no fear at all. The resurrection is what life and death are all about. The resurrection of Jesus Christ makes all the difference in the world.

TODAY'S BIBLE CHALLENGE

1. In Paul's account of the resurrection in 1 Corinthians 15, who was the first person Jesus appeared to?
2. How many brothers and sisters did Jesus appear to after the resurrection?
3. Who is the last enemy to be destroyed?
4. What cannot inherit the kingdom of God?
5. At the sound of what instrument will we all be changed?

WEEK 7

Get All Your Burial Needs at Laz-R-Us

Read John 11:1–44. • • • •

Nobody likes to hear his name called. Not by teachers. Not by the IRS. Not by the pastor, especially during the sermon as an example of how not to live.

One time I was in the Tel Aviv airport in Israel, and my name came over the loud speaker. I froze. Apparently they were watching me and wondered why I wandered from my group. "They were moving too slowly," I replied. The officials didn't like the answer.

Two hours and a full body check later they let me go.

There is one time you want to hear your name called, and that's when Jesus calls you from the grave and into his presence. Martha understood resurrection when her brother, Lazarus, died, saying to Jesus, "I know he will rise again in the resurrection at the last day" (John 11:24). So Jesus gave us a little sneak peek into that last day. Lazarus, playing the dead guy, lay in the tomb when Jesus called his name. "Lazarus," he cried. "Get yourself out here!" Lazarus hopped out, and the people were amazed. All Jesus had to do was say his name, and he was freed from the tomb.

So the question is, does Jesus know your name? Of course he knows everything, but do you have a personal relationship with Jesus Christ? Lazarus was a close friend. Jesus knew his name, but he knew him better as a friend. Jesus calls the names of his friends on that last day. Make sure he knows you, or better yet, make sure you know him.

TODAY'S BIBLE CHALLENGE

1. What village was Lazarus from?
2. How many more days did Jesus stay where he was when he heard Lazarus was sick?
3. How long had Lazarus been in the tomb?
4. How far was Bethany from Jerusalem?
5. Which sister knew Lazarus would rise again in the resurrection at the last day?

Biblical Greeting Cards—Job

Read Job 1. ● ● ● ●

The book of Job tells us that God loves to do protective gardening. How does he do that? He plants a hedge around us. A hedge is a thick brush that makes it difficult for invading armies to plow through and attack their target. God's hedge keeps out the worst enemy of all time—Satan. Satan runs up to the hedge and goes, "Curses, I hate this hedge! Always blocking my plans to ruin someone's life."

When we pray for the hedge of protection, Job 1 tells us it's a real thing. Satan wants access to our lives, but God denies him through a spiritual keep-out zone. He cannot destroy something unless God gives him permission.

And why would God allow Satan access to someone's life?

- To prove a point, as he did with Job, and show Satan that Job would not curse God.
- To strengthen the defenses of the attacked, building up their perseverance (Romans 5:3).
- To turn the sinners over to what they asked for (Romans 1:24).

So thank God for the hedge he has around you, and know that when difficulties invade your life and the hedges have been breached, there must be a good reason.

TODAY'S BIBLE CHALLENGE

1. In what land did Job live?
2. How many children did Job first have?
3. What tribe carried off Job's oxen and donkeys and killed his servants?
4. What burned up Job's sheep?
5. What destroyed Job's house and killed his sons and daughters?

Love Lines—Song of Songs

Read Song of Songs 2. • • • •

Solomon's Song of Songs gives us two important communication skills husbands and wives need to perfect to keep the passion alive in their marriages.

Husbands need to notice their wives specifically. The man in Song of Songs points out particulars about his wife that he loves about her. He doesn't say, "Yeah, you look nice." He is very specific, commenting on her face, voice, hair, teeth, temple, neck, breasts, lips, cheeks, even her smell. Women love details and they want know what it is about that dress that the man likes. Men, there is nothing you can do to make the woman react any differently. You must increase your vocabulary beyond "It's good" and "I like it" to "I like the way it shows off your legs" or "That color really brings out your eyes."

Wives need to build up their men and make them sound like Chuck Norris. The woman in Song of Songs uses words of strength to describe her man. She likens him to a mare, a stag, a chariot, and trees. Many of the comments reveal her submission to him, saying he takes her in his arms, and he carries her away. She appears vulnerable and helpless because of his love. Men like that. They like to know that a woman melts into putty when he's around. Women may have to come up with new compliments when their once-virile man now sports a ten-pound tire around his belly. That's okay, ladies. It's for a good cause.

So men, focus on the specifics.

And women, focus on his strength.

And you both will be making beautiful music together.

TODAY'S BIBLE CHALLENGE

1. In Song of Songs 2, the woman describes herself as what flower?
2. What should the daughters of Jerusalem not arouse or awaken before it so desires?
3. The woman describes the man as like a gazelle or a young what?
4. What animals ruin the vineyard?
5. What flowers does the man browse among?

Real Housewives of the OT—Rebekah

Read Genesis 24:1–31. ● ● ● ●

Imagine your dad sending out the butler to find you a wife. There are a lot of things wrong with this scenario. First of all, it's your dad's bright idea. Then, you are at the mercy of a servant who is trying to pick out someone he thinks your dad thinks would be best for you. Sound like a potential marital disaster?

This is precisely what happened to Isaac, but it worked out perfectly. Why? The quest for the perfect bride began with prayer. The matchmaker prayed for God's divine intervention. He even went so far as to ask for a clear sign. God got involved and offered his best choice.

The woman, Rebekah, was not only beautiful on the outside but on the inside. Men like Samson picked women for their looks. See how that worked out for him. Rebekah was pure, a virgin, indicating her moral standards. The servant wanted a woman who would take the time to help a stranger and his camels, even offering him a place for the night. By coming to the well, Rebekah proved she was a hard worker and responsible.

When looking for the perfect bride, begin with prayer. Ask God to bring her to you at the right time and to the right place. When you find someone, ask some questions:

- Is she beautiful on the outside and inside?
- Is she pure with moral standards?
- Is she hospitable, loving others more than herself?

Who could say no to such a beautiful woman? Isaac couldn't. The Bible's first blind date worked perfectly because God was asked to be the matchmaker.

TODAY'S BIBLE CHALLENGE

1. Abraham made his servant swear Isaac would not marry a daughter from what people group?
2. To what town did the servant travel to find a wife for Isaac?
3. As a sign that Abraham's servant had found the woman for Isaac, what did he pray she would offer to water?
4. What jewelry did Abraham's servant give Rebekah when they first met?
5. Who was Rebekah's brother?

Seven Churches of Revelation

Read Revelation 2. • • • •

How would your church feel if it got a report card from God? You would probably want all As, right? And positive marks in the comments section. No absences, of course. How fulfilling it would be if God said he saw our hard work and our perseverance. We would love it if God applauded our resistance to the evil practices and twisted theology trying to creep into our teachings. Our congregation would feel strengthened if God told us he was fighting to keep our doors open.

Then again, it's hard to imagine God writing negative comments, calling our church dead and our deeds unfinished and telling us we need to repent. How devastating to have God tell us that we have fallen out of love with him.

Seven churches, all in the area of modern-day Turkey, got their report cards in the final book of the Bible. Some of the grades that these seven churches received appear to be As, with a B and a C mixed in. However two churches (Sardis and Laodicea) got Fs, with nothing good written on their report cards.

While none of us strives for an F, we shouldn't be happy with Bs and Cs either. Only an A grade is worthy of the perfect, sinless God. If he is perfect and the church is his representative on earth, then the church should strive to be perfect too. How would God grade your church?

TODAY'S BIBLE CHALLENGE

1. How many stars and lampstands are mentioned in Revelation 2?
2. What group's practices did the church of Ephesus hate?
3. In Revelation 2, who has a throne in Pergamum?
4. What faithful witness was put to death in Pergamum?
5. Who is the woman that the church in Thyatira tolerated?

Ezekiel Bread

Read Ezekiel 4. • • • •

It's not easy being a prophet.

God wanted his exiled people in Babylon to learn a lesson during their seventy-year hiatus away from the promised land, so that when they returned, they would not make the same mistakes twice.

God pounded Ezekiel with wild visions and incredible tasks, making him do some extraordinary stunts to get the Israelites' attention. In chapter 4, he built a model of Jerusalem then lay down on his left side for 390 days (to represent the ten nations of Israel) and on his right for 40 days (to represent the two nations of Judah). That's 430 days lying on the ground. That's one year and two months. God then gave Ezekiel a recipe of six ingredients for bread, a pure and healthy list of all-natural products that is even used today. However, God asked Ezekiel to cook the bread over . . . human excrement. This all-natural biodegradable fuel immediately contaminates whatever is cooked over it, especially for a Jew on a strict kosher diet.

But that's the point God wanted to make. "My people," God was saying through this demonstration with Ezekiel, "I offer you something pure and healthy, and yet you contaminate it with your human wastefulness." As soon as man decides to add his own ingredients to God's perfect recipe, the whole thing turns to . . . well, you get the idea.

God doesn't mince words with Ezekiel or with us. When dealing with God's plan, we have to remove the human element.

TODAY'S BIBLE CHALLENGE

1. On what did Ezekiel draw the city of Jerusalem?
2. With what did God tell Ezekiel he would tie up the prophet?
3. What six ingredients are in Ezekiel's bread?
4. How much bread did Ezekiel eat every day?
5. Instead of human excrement, what did God allow Ezekiel to bake his bread over?

The Temple

Read 1 Kings 6. ● ● ● ●

In the time of the Old Testament, pagans regularly built temples for their gods. Before Solomon's temple was built in 1 Kings, we read of temples built to Ashtoreth and Dagon. The structure Samson ultimately destroyed in Judges was a temple that doubled as a multilevel stadium.

So it only seemed right that God would ask for a temple to be built for him. But his temple was different from other gods' for a number of reasons. The pagans franchised their temples. Anybody at any time could build a worship center for any god. No written approval necessary. God, though, required only one temple for himself in one place. This kept consistency. Plus, there is only one God so there should only be one temple. Multiple temples communicated multiple gods. God's temple came with a very specific, long list of rules. For God to live in his temple, the people needed to follow God's commands. If they didn't, he moved out and the blessings dried up. God does not make his home in a place of disobedience.

God asked for a home where he could establish his kingdom. This home was the kingdom of Israel, and through this nation would come the King of the Jews, who would establish the kingdom of God throughout the earth. Temples were places of sacrifice. Once Jesus arrived, the temple was no longer needed for sacrifices. Its purpose became obsolete because Jesus sacrificed once for all.

Now God builds his temple in the hearts of people through the Holy Spirit. Bricks and gold are no longer needed. You are the temple, the home of his Holy Spirit.

TODAY'S BIBLE CHALLENGE

1. How many years after the Israelites came out of Egypt did Solomon begin to build the temple?
2. How many years had Solomon been king when he began to build the temple?
3. What sound was not heard while the temple was built?
4. From what tree were the paneling and beams of the temple made?
5. From what wood were the cherubim in the inner sanctuary of the temple made?

WEEK 8

My Tweet Lord—Matthew

Read Matthew 9:9–13. • • • •

Can you believe God called a corrupt tax collector to follow him? That's like God marching into the Capitol building in Washington and asking a shady politician to follow him. Or entering a women's clinic and asking an abortion doctor to follow him. Or busting through an Al Qaeda compound and asking a terrorist to follow him. Or walking onto a studio lot and asking an atheist actor to follow him. Or entering a megachurch and asking a corrupt evangelist to follow him. Or driving to a dealership and inviting a crooked car salesman to follow him. Or stepping onto a stage and asking a rapper of explicit lyrics to follow him. Or slipping into a strip club and asking a dancer to follow him.

If God called Matthew, he could call anybody. Only those who thought they were good enough to be called God's chosen questioned Jesus' choice of friends. "It is not the healthy who need a doctor, but the sick" (Matthew 9:12), Jesus replied. Jesus didn't come to call those good enough. The choices were rather slim. So he called those who needed healing and were willing to get better. That means he could call anyone, even you and me.

TODAY'S BIBLE CHALLENGE

1. Where was Matthew sitting when Jesus called?
2. What two groups of people were eating with Jesus and the disciples at Matthew's house?
3. Jesus told the Pharisees he desired mercy but not what?
4. Jesus told the Pharisees he did not come to call the righteous but whom?
5. According to Luke 5:27, what other name was Matthew known by?

Biblical Rednecks—Sister, Sister

Read Genesis 12. ● ● ● ●

So what was the problem with Abram telling the Pharaoh of Egypt that his wife was his sister? And then doing it again with Abimelech (Genesis 20)? Selfishness. Abram really protected only himself by deceiving the Egyptians about his relationship with Sarai. He felt they would kill him to take his wife, yet if they thought she was his sister, they would just take her and let him live. Sarai loses in both scenarios. Abram showed his true self.

Abram also showed his mistrust of God. In Genesis 12, God called him to the promised land, where God said he would make Abram into a great nation. Yet when a famine hit, driving the family to the fertile crescent of Egypt, Abram figured all promises were off. Instead of asking God what to do, he created a crazy scheme.

Then in Genesis 20, after more direct promises from God to bless him, Abram (now known as Abraham) did the same exact thing again in the Philistine city of Gerar. Abraham figured this lie worked before, so why not again? He should have trusted God to keep them alive. Abraham justified the lie this time by saying Sarai (now known as Sarah) was his half-sister, from the same father but a different mother. While that technically was true, Abraham deceived others for personal gain. So for the reasons of self-preservation, selfishness, and mistrust of God, Abraham deceived two kings. Whether the fact technically was true made no difference. We never have to deceive man when we have the promises of God.

TODAY'S BIBLE CHALLENGE

1. How old was Abram when he followed the Lord's call to the land God would show him?
2. From what region did Abram leave?
3. Who went with Abram to Canaan?
4. Who praised Sarai's beauty to Pharaoh?
5. What did Pharaoh give Abram in return for Sarai?

Jesus Christ Superstar Wars—Paddan Aram

Read Genesis 28. ● ● ● ●

Paddan Aram could be called the birthplace of the Israelites. It is the region where Terah, Abraham's father, settled in the city of Haran after leaving Ur. Abraham wanted his son to marry within the family, so he sent his servant to Paddan Aram, modern-day Syria, to find that perfect descendant. Isaac found his Rebekah in Paddan Aram. His son, Jacob, went to Paddan Aram to marry Rachel (and Leah too). Twelve of his children were born there.

Paddan Aram eventually produced a group of people known as the Arameans. Biblical history describes the Arameans as a tough and persistent enemy of Israel. What happened that changed this region from a home of the family to the home of the enemy? The relationship between Paddan Aram and Israel was no longer about legacy and genealogy, but borders and power. Time blurred the honored past and focused on the selfish future.

The same thing happens in our families today. Fights break out between family members, destroying the bonds that held them together for decades. Whether it's a slow drift or a sudden tearing, family lines need constant attention and hard work to stay together for centuries to come.

TODAY'S BIBLE CHALLENGE

1. Jacob went to Paddan Aram to find a wife among the daughters of whom?
2. Who heard that Isaac sent Jacob to Paddan Aram to find a wife and responded by marrying someone from the line of Ishmael?
3. Who was ascending and descending the stairway to heaven in Jacob's dream on his way to Paddan Aram?
4. What did Jacob call the place where he saw the stairway to heaven?
5. What was the city formerly called that Jacob renamed?

Kids Sayeth the Cutest Things— Shadrach, Meshach, Abednego

Read Daniel 3. ● ● ● ●

Is life turning up the heat? Imagine how Shadrach, Meshach, and Abednego felt. Their survival in the fiery furnace tells us how we can survive when things get hot.

1. Don't run away from the fire. Accused of worshiping God despite public policy that said they must worship only the image of gold, Shadrach, Meshach, and Abednego defied the world for their love of God. They didn't fear the fire. They embraced it.

2. The enemy will get burned, but not those who worship God. The soldiers who carried the trio into the fire died trying to kill Shadrach, Meshach, and Abednego. The enemy's own devices backfired and burned them.

3. God can burn off the ropes that bind you, so you can walk around freely while everything around you turns to ashes. He can free you and protect you at the hottest point of any crisis.

4. God is there with you in the fire. Nebuchadnezzar saw four men walking around in the fire. The fourth had to be either an angel or Jesus himself. God doesn't leave you when things get hot. He jumps in with you.

5. God may throw you in the fire to keep others out of the fire. Nebuchadnezzar praised the true God after seeing the faithful trio survive the furnace. The world watches the faithful go through tough times and in turn accepts God as Lord and Savior. This eventually keeps them from the eternal fire that never goes out. It's the only fire no one survives and the ultimate fire God wants to save everyone from.

TODAY'S BIBLE CHALLENGE

1. How tall was the image Nebuchadnezzar made?
2. What did Nebuchadnezzar decree should happen every time people heard the music play?
3. How much hotter did Nebuchadnezzar heat the fire to burn Daniel's friends?
4. What did Nebuchadnezzar say the fourth man in the fire looked like?
5. When Shadrach, Meshach, and Abednego stepped out of the furnace, what did they not smell like?

Thou Shall Not Covet

Read Exodus 20. ● ● ● ●

Coveting is desire. It means "I want" or "Give me that" or "How come they get nice things but I don't?" But it's also wanting something so badly that you forget what you really need. It's a passionate must-have.

Coveting is dissatisfaction. It's saying, "My life is worthless unless I have my neighbor's ox. His ox is so awesome. Mine is an old model and emits gas." Coveting causes you to hate what God has blessed you with and feel jealousy for what God has given your neighbor.

Coveting is infatuation. It's loving something that looks good from a distance. Your neighbor's wife may look beautiful on the outside tying up hay bales and picking the peas, but inside the house she could be a bossy, naggy, foul-mouthed hag who can't even cook those peas. We fall in love with what we see, but we don't really know what we'll get.

Coveting is tunnel-vision blindness. We become so focused on our neighbor's donkey that we forget we have a donkey too. We can't see what we have because we're staring at what our neighbor has.

God says through this commandment, "Stop looking at what you don't have, and start appreciating what you do have." Coveting tells God you think he's not doing a good job providing for you. So thank him for your donkey, and stop looking at your neighbor's ox.

TODAY'S BIBLE CHALLENGE

1. In the second commandment, God said we should not make an image in the form of anything found in what three places?
2. In the second commandment, God said he is jealous and punishes children for the sin of their parents to what generations?
3. What day did the commandments say the Lord blessed and made holy?
4. Which commandment says that we will live long in the land the Lord gave us if we follow it?
5. Which animals did the tenth commandment specifically say we should not covet?

Armor of God

Read Ephesians 6. ● ● ● ●

To go into battle without any armor is either really stupid or really brave. For a warrior to go armorless, he would need to have complete trust in his own skills or complete trust in God's protection. David knew his own skills with the sling to take down lions and bears, but he had faith that his battle against the Philistine was God's to win, so he refused to wear Saul's armor. Saul's armor couldn't even protect Saul when the archers overwhelmed him in 1 Samuel 31. Arrows find a way to sneak through the weak spots in armor.

To walk out into life without any spiritual armor is just plain stupid. The devil is an experienced warrior who knows how to take down the most faithful. We are fighting an invisible enemy. Try swinging a sword at that! This enemy spies on us, watches our every move, knows where our eyes wander, hears our whispers. We are at a disadvantage if we try to defeat that enemy by ourselves.

We need to arm ourselves. Notice Ephesians tells us to put on the full armor of God. Not a couple pieces here and there. Truth, righteousness, readiness, salvation, and the word of God cover every weakness in us by displaying God's strength. The armor does not miraculously appear on our bodies. A conscious effort is required to put the pieces in place. We have to accept it, ask for it, cover ourselves in it, and trust it.

Get ready to rumble, but don't enter the battlefield naked.

TODAY'S BIBLE CHALLENGE

1. Which commandment is the first to come with a promise?
2. Whom should fathers not exasperate?
3. Which piece of the armor is buckled around your waist?
4. What does the shield of faith extinguish?
5. What is the sword of the Spirit?

Bible Bad Guys

Read 1 Kings 21:17–29. • • • •

Here's a quick lesson on how to be a Bible Bad Guy.

1. Try to disrupt God's plans with your own selfish desires.
2. Worship other gods besides the one true God.
3. Attack God's people.
4. Ignore God's warnings.

If you've done those four things, then congratulations—you're a Bible Bad Guy.

King Ahab of Israel was the most wanted of the Bible Bad Guys.

1. He reigned as the champion, doing more evil than any king before him.
2. He provoked God by worshiping the gods Baal and Asherah.
3. He looked the other way while God's prophets were massacred.
4. He ignored the prophets who didn't tell him what he wanted to hear.

But God loves even the baddest of the bad. Ahab repented after Elijah's warning, and God backed off on his immediate judgment (although imminent judgment remained). You can't be so bad that God can't love you. Even the worst of the worst get a glimpse of grace.

TODAY'S BIBLE CHALLENGE

1. Who was Ahab's father?
2. How many years did Ahab reign?
3. What weather catastrophe did Elijah predict during Ahab's reign?
4. In 1 Kings 20, what king of Aram did King Ahab defeat?
5. What king killed everyone in the house of Ahab living in Jezreel?

WEEK 9

Jericho—Good Contractors Are Hard to Find

Read Joshua 6. ● ● ● ●

God gave some interesting instructions to the Israelites in order to defeat the city of Jericho. First they marched around the city once a day for six days. The priests blew the trumpets while the tribe was told not to say a word, but to march in silence. On the seventh day, they marched around Jericho seven times, and on the seventh time the people shouted. As they gave that shout, the walls collapsed and the Israelites stormed the city.

We know what the Israelites did that week, but what was it like for the people of Jericho? At first the whole marching-around-the-city act probably seemed ridiculous. "What are they up to?" By day two or three it probably caused a snicker and some sarcastic words: "Is this all they can do? Maybe they're getting dizzy." By day four or five, the Jericho citizens may have felt the whole thing was kind of creepy: "Okay, this is weird! They're scaring the children!" By day six, it all got just plain annoying: "Won't they just go away?" By day seven, their entire world collapsed.

Why did God ask the Israelites to go through all these steps before destroying the city? God may have been warning the innocent of Jericho to pack up and leave. The entire seven-day mini-siege gave the inhabitants time to repent and discover the one true God.

They missed an opportunity of grace by responding with sarcasm or fear.

God extends his love to the people of the world. They just need to see the signs and get in line.

TODAY'S BIBLE CHALLENGE

1. What did the priests carry in front of the ark?
2. How many priests marched in front of the ark?
3. What three types of animals did the invading army kill?
4. Joshua pronounced a curse on anyone who tried to do what to Jericho?
5. What did Joshua say would occur to anyone who tried to rebuild Jericho?

Lyrical Miracles—Smoke and Fire

Read Exodus 13:17–22. ● ● ● ●

When God led the Israelites toward the promised land, he did so with a pillar of smoke during the day and a pillar of fire by night. This incredible visual manifestation never left its place in front of the group. God wanted them to know that he was with them, that he would never leave them, and that he had a very specific path for them to travel.

Do you think there were any Israelites who were nonbelievers? If you asked any of them during their exodus, "Does God exist?" they would have pointed to the pillar of smoke and fire and said, "Yeah, he's right there." Then how come these same Israelites made a golden calf, disobeyed God's commands by stealing, and got upset at God's mouthpiece, Moses? They saw the God of smoke and fire, but they didn't like what that God had to say. They did not make that God of smoke and fire the God of their lives. If he told them to do something they didn't want to do, they looked away and preferred their selfish gods.

Obviously believing has nothing to do with seeing and everything to do with trusting. If God manifested himself in front of you, you'd be amazed, but would you do whatever he asked you to do? Obedience is true belief.

TODAY'S BIBLE CHALLENGE

1. Whose bones did Moses take as the Israelites left Egypt?
2. What did the pillars of cloud and fire allow the Israelites to do?
3. In Exodus 14, the Lord looked down from the pillar of fire and confused what army?
4. When the pillar of cloud stood at the entrance to the Tent of Meeting in Exodus 33, what did all the Israelites do?
5. In Numbers 12:5, when the pillar of cloud rested at the entrance of the tent, whom did the Lord summon?

Biblical Rednecks—David Dancing

Read 2 Samuel 6. ● ● ● ●

Dancing half-naked may be one of those moments a president or king would hate to see playing over and over on YouTube. Some have lost their leadership positions because they were caught in such compromising positions. For David this was the moment that people wondered, "Is that any way for a king to act? Dancing around with his shirt off like that?" David didn't care. He was filled with joy.

Have you ever had one of those moments when you were so overcome with emotion that you danced like a fool? Many of us don't. We're afraid that it will hurt our images or others will laugh at us. We're afraid of cameras and instant uploads to Facebook.

But if you were a part of a moment promised by God, fulfilled before your eyes, would you dance? How about that soon-coming moment when not just the ark but the people of God will enter the promised land of heaven with their resurrected bodies? Think there will be a little dancing going on? A box step? Salsa? Electric slide? You bet there will be.

So there's no reason you can't start practicing your dance moves now for the big marathon coming soon. It'll last for eternity, and we'll all be making fools of ourselves.

TODAY'S BIBLE CHALLENGE

1. What kind of cart brought the ark of God toward Jerusalem?
2. Before David brought the ark to Jerusalem, at whose houses did the ark rest?
3. Who reached out and took hold of the ark and died?
4. When the ark arrived in Jerusalem and David had finished sacrificing, what did he give to everyone?
5. Because of Michal's reaction to David, what happened to her?

CSI Holy Land—Eglon

Read Judges 3:12–30. • • • •

During a tumultuous time in Israel's history, at the beginning of their occupation of the promised land, leadership was nonexistent. God turned to judges to bring judgment on the enemies, delivering God's people from oppression. King Eglon, a Moabite working with the Ammonites and Amalekites, became that kind of abusive leader for eighteen years.

The Israelites cried out to God for help, so he sent them Ehud, who had a surprisingly important characteristic: left-handedness. We would expect God to send someone skilled in martial arts or slingshot shooting, but no, God chose Ehud based on what hand he used to throw a baseball.

While it may not seem like much at first, left-handed people are pretty sneaky during battle, just as left-handed pitchers can strike out right-handed batters and left-handed boxers can be effective against right-handed opponents. Right handers, in that day, kept their eye on their opponent's deadly right hand. A left hand comes out of nowhere.

It's also possible that when entering a king's court, people were frisked for weapons on their inside left thigh, the ideal place a right-hander straps his sword. Ehud could have eluded security by strapping his weapon on the right thigh. Ehud saved his people because he used the wrong hand. But for God it was the right one.

You may think you're too short or too slow. You may regret being a bad singer or terrible writer. You may wish God had made you prettier or more coordinated. But you know what? God made you unique for a purpose. You may not think God could ever use you, but he can.

TODAY'S BIBLE CHALLENGE

1. What tribe was Ehud from?
2. What did Ehud say to Eglon to make the king follow him into the secluded room?
3. Where did Ehud plunge the sword into Eglon?
4. What did the servants think Eglon was doing to make them wait before checking on him?
5. Ehud led a charge against the Moabites that killed how many?

Daniel's Visions

Read Daniel 7. ● ● ● ●

Daniel saw some weird things in his day. His visions perplexed not only him but modern-day quasi-prophets who think they have unlocked the mysteries of what Daniel saw. What was the purpose of the visions?

Daniel admitted that the visions troubled and disturbed him, but God did his best to comfort Daniel. God immediately interpreted the visions and gave Daniel answers. God wanted to show Daniel that God had answers for the questions to come. And God's explanations were logical. While the answers would be devastating, Daniel received clear interpretation. God didn't want him living in mystery. That's not God's desire. He's the God of light and truth. Confusion and chaos are Satan's MO.

God used the visions so Daniel could see and feel the evil of what was going to happen. God used sensory cues to help Daniel express what was to come. God showed Daniel who these leaders really were—beasts with sharp teeth and claws who only wanted to devour and kill. He could have said to Daniel, "Hey, let me tell you about all the bad kingdoms that will oppress Israel," but instead he allowed Daniel to experience their horror. These were not literal mythological creatures, just visual metaphors. God allowed Daniel to feel the fear, but he wanted Daniel's comfort and strength to rely only on him.

God knows the unknown is scary for us, but God knows the future. He has it all figured out.

TODAY'S BIBLE CHALLENGE

1. In Daniel's vision what came out of the sea?
2. What did the bear in Daniel's dream have in its mouth?
3. How many horns did the fourth beast start out with in Daniel's dream?
4. What did the four great beasts represent?
5. What did the ten horns represent?

Elijah/Elisha Miracles

Read 2 Kings 2:1–14. • • • •

Did Elisha want to be a prophet? You bet he did.

When Elijah approached Elisha to replace him, Elisha torched his plow and used the fire to cook the meat from the ox attached to it, serving steak to whoever was hungry. No more plowing for him. It was time for a career change.

Then word got out that Elijah was going to soon depart. Elisha knew this would happen, yet everything Elijah told him to do Elisha obeyed. He could have said, "You're history, old man. I'm the next big thing," but he respected his mentor to the end. As Elijah prepared one last miracle before he left, he asked Elisha what he wanted. Elisha wanted double his master's power. What an honor Elijah must have felt, knowing his legacy would continue in the life of Elisha better than before.

Elisha never turned back. He stayed loyal to the end. He wanted to be twice as influential as his master. He wanted to be a prophet and was willing to be mentored to achieve that goal. He showed respect and humility and was rewarded with an influential and fruitful life.

Are you willing to humble yourself before a teacher so God can teach you? Are you ready to be twice the person you could ever imagine to be?

TODAY'S BIBLE CHALLENGE

1. In 2 Kings 2, what two cities did Elijah travel to?
2. Who went out and met Elisha at every place they visited?
3. What did Elijah strike the water with?
4. What happened to the water when Elijah struck it?
5. What pulled the chariot that took Elijah away?

Book of Romans

Read Romans 8:14–30. • • • •

One of Rome's greatest contributions to the world during their empire's reign was the construction of roads. Estimates attribute to Rome nearly two hundred fifty thousand miles of roads, connecting countries and making travel easier.

One of Paul's greatest contributions to our faith is the Roman Road, a series of verses in his letter to the Romans that explains clearly the need for a relationship with Jesus Christ:

- "For all have sinned and fall short of the glory of God" (3:23). We all have a sin problem.
- "For the wages of sin is death, but the gift of God is eternal life in Christ Jesus our Lord" (6:23). We will die because of our sins unless we turn to Christ.
- "But God demonstrates his own love for us in this: While we were still sinners, Christ died for us" (5:8). The solution to our sin problem is God's love.
- "If you declare with your mouth, 'Jesus is Lord,' and believe in your heart that God raised him from the dead, you will be saved" (10:9). We must declare and believe to be saved.
- "Everyone who calls on the name of the Lord will be saved" (10:13). We must cry out to God for help.

- "Therefore, there is now no condemnation for those who are in Christ Jesus" (8:1). Because of our relationship with Christ, we are no longer penalized with death because of our sins.

This is the greatest road we can ever travel down. Have you walked this Roman Road in your life?

TODAY'S BIBLE CHALLENGE

1. What does the Spirit testify with our spirit in Romans 8?
2. For us to share in Christ's glory, we must share in his what?
3. What was subjected to frustration?
4. Paul wrote that creation has been groaning like the pains experienced during what?
5. What helps us in our weakness?

ANSWERS TO THE DAILY BIBLE CHALLENGES

WEEK 1

Day 1: What Do You *Noah* About the Ark?

   1. cypress (Genesis 6:14)

   2. three (Genesis 6:16)

   3. seven (Genesis 7:2)

   4. six hundred years old (Genesis 7:6)

   5. eight (Genesis 7:13)

Day 2: Faithbook—A Friend Request
  from the Burning Bush

   1. Jethro's (Exodus 3:1)

   2. Horeb, the mountain of God (Exodus 3:1)

   3. "Moses! Moses!" (Exodus 3:4)

   4. his sandals (Exodus 3:5)

   5. milk and honey (Exodus 3:8)

Day 3: In the Name of the Lord of the Rings

1. four (Exodus 39:10)
2. the twelve sons of Israel (Exodus 39:14)
3. pomegranates (Exodus 39:24)
4. bells (Exodus 39:25)
5. "HOLY TO THE LORD" (Exodus 39:30)

Day 4: Kids Sayeth the Cutest Things—Jonah

1. Joppa (Jonah 1:3)
2. his own god (Jonah 1:5)
3. cargo (Jonah 1:5)
4. they cast lots (Jonah 1:7)
5. pick him up and throw him into the sea (Jonah 1:12)

Day 5: Swords at the Last Supper Table

1. the day of Unleavened Bread (Luke 22:7)
2. Peter and John (Luke 22:8)
3. jar of water (Luke 22:10)
4. all the apostles (Luke 22:14, 31)
5. who was greatest (Luke 22:24)

Day 6: The Finger of God

1. Noah (Genesis 8:20–21)
2. hearing (God heard) and sight (God looked) (Exodus 2:24–25)
3. his face (Exodus 33:20)
4. his hand (Exodus 33:22)
5. his back (Exodus 33:23)

Day 7: Women of the Bible
1. Zilpah (Genesis 30:10–13)
2. Elisha (2 Kings 4:32–35)
3. Mary Magdalene (John 20:16, 18)
4. Lydia (Acts 16:14)
5. Priscilla (Acts 18:2, 18)

WEEK 2

Day 1: My Tweet Lord—Sarah
1. near the great trees of Mamre (Genesis 18:1)
2. three (Genesis 18:2)
3. bread (Genesis 18:6)
4. at the entrance to the tent (Genesis 18:10)
5. laughing (Genesis 18:15)

Day 2: The Eye of the Tebow
1. Euodia and Syntyche (Philippians 4:2)
2. rejoice in the Lord (Philippians 4:4)
3. the peace of God (Philippians 4:7)
4. content (Philippians 4:11)
5. strength (Philippians 4:13)

Day 3: Kids Sayeth the Cutest Things—
Moses in the Basket
1. three months (Exodus 2:2)
2. his sister (Exodus 2:4)
3. Moses' mother (Exodus 2:7–8)
4. Pharaoh's daughter (Exodus 2:10)
5. because she "drew him out of the water" (Exodus 2:10)

Day 4: CSI Holy Land—Jezebel

1. one hundred (1 Kings 18:4)
2. Naboth (1 Kings 21:7, 13)
3. Elijah (1 Kings 21:17–19)
4. eye makeup (2 Kings 9:30)
5. eunuchs (2 Kings 9:32–33)

Day 5: The Beatitudes

1. those who mourn (Matthew 5:4)
2. the earth (Matthew 5:5)
3. the pure in heart (Matthew 5:8)
4. the peacemakers (Matthew 5:9)
5. the prophets (Matthew 5:12)

Day 6: The Parables

1. a priest and a Levite (Luke 10:31–32)
2. three loaves of bread (Luke 11:5)
3. 450 gallons of olive oil (Luke 16:6)
4. a judge (Luke 18:2)
5. robbers, evildoers, adulterers (Luke 18:11)

Day 7: Animals of the Bible

1. a deer (Psalm 18:33)
2. the goat (Isaiah 11:6)
3. the ox (Daniel 4:33)
4. false prophets (Matthew 7:15)
5. Jesus (John 1:29)

WEEK 3

Day 1: The Parable of the Son Who
Moved Back in with His Parents
1. pigs (Luke 15:16)
2. his father's hired servants (Luke 15:17)
3. robe, ring, sandals (Luke 15:22)
4. music and dancing (Luke 15:25)
5. prostitutes (Luke 15:30)

Day 2: Faithbook—Gideon
1. Jerub-Baal (Judges 7:1)
2. twenty-two thousand (Judges 7:3)
3. three hundred (Judges 7:6)
4. a round loaf of barley bread (Judges 7:13)
5. Oreb and Zeeb (Judges 7:25)

Day 3: Genesis or Genesis
1. Eliezer of Damascus (Genesis 15:2)
2. the stars (Genesis 15:5)
3. a heifer, a goat and a ram, each three years old, along
   with a dove and a young pigeon (Genesis 15:9)
4. birds of prey (Genesis 15:11)
5. four hundred (Genesis 15:13)

Day 4: Kids Sayeth the Cutest Things—
David and Goliath
1. his staff (1 Samuel 17:40)
2. sword and spear and javelin (1 Samuel 17:45)

3. the Philistine's (1 Samuel 17:51)

4. Jerusalem (1 Samuel 17:54)

5. in his own tent (1 Samuel 17:54)

Day 5: Genealogy of Jesus

1. Abraham (Matthew 1:2)

2. Tamar (Matthew 1:3)

3. Obed (Matthew 1:5)

4. Jacob (Matthew 1:16)

5. fourteen (Matthew 1:17)

Day 6: It's Time

1. die (Ecclesiastes 3:2)

2. heal (Ecclesiastes 3:3)

3. laugh (Ecclesiastes 3:4)

4. give up (Ecclesiastes 3:6)

5. hate (Ecclesiastes 3:8)

Day 7: Proverbs

1. the fear of the LORD (Proverbs 1:7)

2. his father and mother (Proverbs 1:8)

3. wisdom (Proverbs 1:20)

4. the adulteress (Proverbs 2:16–18)

5. they will be filled to overflowing (Proverbs 3:9–10)

WEEK 4

Day 1: Jesus Picked Up the Tab

1. towel (John 13:4)

2. his hands and his head (John 13:9)

3. a piece of bread (John 13:26)

4. Judas (John 13:29)

5. the rooster (John 13:38)

Day 2: Biblical Greeting Cards—Lot

1. Zoar (Genesis 19:23–24)

2. burning sulfur (Genesis 19:23)

3. Lot's sons-in-law (Genesis 19:14)

4. Moab (Genesis 19:37)

5. Ben-Ammi (Genesis 19:38)

Day 3: Set Phasers to Bless—Zadok

1. the ark of the covenant of God (2 Samuel 15:24)

2. Gihon (1 Kings 1:33–35)

3. Solomon (1 Kings 1:39)

4. Ahimaaz (2 Samuel 18:19–33)

5. Ezekiel (Ezekiel 43:19)

Day 4: Lyrical Miracles—Amazing Grace

1. our transgressions (Ephesians 2:5)

2. boast (Ephesians 2:9)

3. good works (Ephesians 2:10)

4. the blood of Christ (Ephesians 2:13)

5. peace (Ephesians 2:17)

Day 5: Languages at Pentecost

1. the blowing of a violent wind (Acts 2:2)

2. house (Acts 2:2)

3. Galilee (Acts 2:7)

4. wine (Acts 2:13)

5. Joel (Acts 2:16)

Day 6: Small but Wise

1. "Give! Give!" (Proverbs 30:15)

2. they store up their food in summer (Proverbs 30:24–25)

3. the crags (Proverbs 30:26)

4. a king (Proverbs 30:27)

5. in kings' palaces (Proverbs 30:28)

Day 7: Peter, Paul, and Mary

1. three thousand (Acts 2:41)

2. three months (Luke 1:56)

3. Acts (Acts 1:14)

4. Tarsus (Acts 9:11)

5. he got up and was baptized (Acts 9:18)

WEEK 5

Day 1: My Tweet Lord—Barabbas

1. Jesus Barabbas (Matthew 27:16)

2. Pilate (Matthew 27:24, 26)

3. Pilate's wife (Matthew 27:19)

4. "Crucify him!" (Matthew 27:23)

5. all the people in the crowd (Matthew 27:25)

Day 2: Lyrical Miracles—Zacchaeus

1. Jericho (Luke 19:1)

2. chief tax collector (Luke 19:2)

3. sycamore-fig tree (Luke 19:4)

4. four (Luke 19:8)

5. salvation (Luke 19:9)

Day 3: Biblical Classified Ads—Aaron's Staff

1. a snake (Exodus 7:10)

2. Nile turned to blood, frogs, gnats (Exodus 7:17–8:19)

3. the leader of each of their ancestral tribes (Numbers 17:2)

4. the name of the tribal leader (Numbers 17:2)

5. the ark of the covenant law (Numbers 17:4)

Day 4: Smote by an Angel—Herod

1. his angel (Acts 12:11)

2. the guards (Acts 12:19)

3. the people of Tyre and Sidon (Acts 12:20)

4. his royal robes (Acts 12:21)

5. continued to spread and flourish (Acts 12:24)

Day 5: False Gods

1. Asherah (Deuteronomy 7:5)

2. Dagon (1 Samuel 5:4)

3. Chemosh (1 Kings 11:7)

4. Molek (1 Kings 11:7)

5. Artemis (Acts 19:24)

Day 6: I Am

1. feeding of the five thousand (John 6:25–35)

2. Moses (John 6:32–33)

3. the sheep (John 10:7)
4. wolf (John 10:11–12)
5. Lazarus (John 11:17–25)

Day 7: Daniel

1. some of the articles from the temple of God (Daniel 1:2)
2. three (Daniel 1:5)
3. Hananiah, Mishael, and Azariah (Daniel 1:6)
4. Belteshazzar (Daniel 1:7)
5. Cyrus (Daniel 1:21)

WEEK 6

Day 1: Man Has Fallen and He Can't Get Up

1. in the middle of the garden (Genesis 3:3)
2. they were opened (Genesis 3:7)
3. fig (Genesis 3:7)
4. in the cool of the day (Genesis 3:8)
5. thorns and thistles (Genesis 3:18)

Day 2: Mad Verses—Proverbs 3:5–6

1. life (Proverbs 3:2)
2. our bones (Proverbs 3:7–8)
3. our barns (Proverbs 3:9–10)
4. wisdom (Proverbs 3:19)
5. our neighbor (Proverbs 3:28)

Day 3: Love Lines—Song of Songs

1. wine (Song of Songs 1:2)
2. Kedar (Song of Songs 1:5)

3. because she's dark (Song of Songs 1:6)

4. earrings (Song of Songs 1:11)

5. doves (Song of Songs 1:15)

Day 4: CSI Holy Land—Joseph

1. seventeen (Genesis 37:2)

2. grain (Genesis 37:7)

3. the sun and moon and eleven stars (Genesis 37:9)

4. Reuben (Genesis 37:21)

5. Judah (Genesis 37:26–27)

Day 5: Feeding the Five Thousand

1. more than half a year's wages (Mark 6:37)

2. five (Mark 6:38)

3. two (Mark 6:38)

4. hundreds and fifties (Mark 6:39–40)

5. men (Mark 6:44)

Day 6: One Hundred Fifty Years Old

1. Seth (Genesis 5:4)

2. Enosh (Genesis 5:6)

3. Adam (Genesis 5:5, 8, 11)

4. Enoch (Genesis 5:24)

5. Lamech (Genesis 5:28–29)

Day 7: The Resurrection

1. Cephas (1 Corinthians 15:5)

2. more than five hundred (1 Corinthians 15:6)

3. death (1 Corinthians 15:26)

4. flesh and blood (1 Corinthians 15:50)

5. the last trumpet (1 Corinthians 15:52)

WEEK 7

Day 1: Get All Your Burial Needs at Laz-R-Us

1. Bethany (John 11:1)

2. two (John 11:6)

3. four days (John 11:17)

4. less than two miles (John 11:18)

5. Martha (John 11:24)

Day 2: Biblical Greeting Cards—Job

1. Uz (Job 1:1)

2. seven sons and three daughters (Job 1:2)

3. Sabeans (Job 1:14–15)

4. the fire of God falling from the heavens (Job 1:16)

5. mighty wind (Job 1:19)

Day 3: Love Lines—Song of Songs

1. a rose of Sharon (Song of Songs 2:1)

2. love (Song of Songs 2:7)

3. stag (Song of Songs 2:9)

4. little foxes (Song of Songs 2:15)

5. the lilies (Song of Songs 2:16)

Day 4: Real Housewives of the OT—Rebekah

1. the Canaanites (Genesis 24:3)

2. Nahor (Genesis 24:10)

3. the camels (Genesis 24:14)

4. a gold nose ring and two gold bracelets (Genesis 24:22)

5. Laban (Genesis 24:29)

Day 5: Seven Churches of Revelation

1. seven (Revelation 2:1)

2. the Nicolaitans (Revelation 2:6)

3. Satan (Revelation 2:12–13)

4. Antipas (Revelation 2:12–13)

5. Jezebel (Revelation 2:18–20)

Day 6: Ezekiel Bread

1. a block of clay (Ezekiel 4:1)

2. ropes (Ezekiel 4:8)

3. wheat and barley, beans and lentils, millet and spelt (Ezekiel 4:9)

4. twenty shekels (Ezekiel 4:10)

5. cow dung (Ezekiel 4:15)

Day 7: The Temple

1. 480 years (1 Kings 6:1)

2. four (1 Kings 6:1)

3. hammer, chisel, or any other iron tool (1 Kings 6:7)

4. cedar (1 Kings 6:10, 15)

5. olive wood (1 Kings 6:23)

WEEK 8

Day 1: My Tweet Lord—Matthew

1. at the tax collector's booth (Matthew 9:9)

2. tax collectors and sinners (Matthew 9:10)

3. sacrifice (Matthew 9:13)
4. sinners (Matthew 9:13)
5. Levi (Luke 5:27)

Day 2: Biblical Rednecks—Sister, Sister

1. seventy-five years old (Genesis 12:4)
2. Harran (Genesis 12:4)
3. his wife Sarai, his nephew Lot, and the people they had acquired in Harran (Genesis 12:5)
4. Pharaoh's officials (Genesis 12:15)
5. sheep and cattle, male and female donkeys, male and female servants, and camels (Genesis 12:16)

Day 3: Jesus Christ Superstar Wars—Paddan Aram

1. Laban (Genesis 28:2)
2. Esau (Genesis 28:6–9)
3. the angels of God (Genesis 28:12)
4. Bethel (Genesis 28:19)
5. Luz (Genesis 28:19)

Day 4: Kids Sayeth the Cutest Things— Shadrach, Meshach, Abednego

1. sixty cubits (Daniel 3:1)
2. they must fall down and worship the image of gold (Daniel 3:5)
3. seven times (Daniel 3:19)
4. a son of the gods (Daniel 3:25)
5. fire (Daniel 3:27)

Day 5: Thou Shall Not Covet

1. in heaven above or on the earth beneath or in the waters below (Exodus 20:4)
2. third and fourth (Exodus 20:5)
3. the Sabbath (Exodus 20:11)
4. honor your father and mother (Exodus 20:12)
5. ox or donkey (Exodus 20:17)

Day 6: Armor of God

1. "Honor your father and mother" (Ephesians 6:2)
2. their children (Ephesians 6:4)
3. the belt of truth (Ephesians 6:14)
4. all the flaming arrows of the evil one (Ephesians 6:16)
5. the word of God (Ephesians 6:17)

Day 7: Bible Bad Guys

1. Omri (1 Kings 16:28)
2. twenty-two years (1 Kings 16:29)
3. drought (1 Kings 17:1)
4. Ben-Hadad (1 Kings 20:32)
5. Jehu (2 Kings 10:11)

WEEK 9

Day 1: Jericho—Good Contractors Are Hard to Find

1. trumpets of rams' horns (Joshua 6:4)
2. seven (Joshua 6:13)
3. cattle, sheep, and donkeys (Joshua 6:21)
4. rebuild it (Joshua 6:26)

5. his firstborn son and his youngest son would die (Joshua 6:26)

Day 2: Lyrical Miracles—Smoke and Fire

1. Joseph's (Exodus 13:19)
2. travel by day or night (Exodus 13:21)
3. the Egyptian army (Exodus 14:24)
4. stand and worship (Exodus 33:10)
5. Aaron and Miriam (Numbers 12:5)

Day 3: Biblical Rednecks—David Dancing

1. a new cart (2 Samuel 6:3)
2. Abinadab and Obed-Edom (2 Samuel 6:3, 12)
3. Uzzah (2 Samuel 6:6–7)
4. a loaf of bread, a cake of raisins, and a cake of dates (2 Samuel 6:19)
5. she had no children to the day of her death (2 Samuel 6:23)

Day 4: CSI Holy Land—Eglon

1. Benjamin (Judges 3:15)
2. "I have a message from God for you" (Judges 3:20)
3. his belly (Judges 3:21)
4. relieving himself (Judges 3:24)
5. ten thousand (Judges 3:29)

Day 5: Daniel's Visions

1. four beasts (Daniel 7:3)
2. three ribs (Daniel 7:5)

3. ten (Daniel 7:7)
4. the four kings that will rise from the earth (Daniel 7:17)
5. ten kings who will come from the fourth kingdom (Daniel 7:24)

Day 6: Elijah/Elisha Miracles

1. Bethel, Jericho (2 Kings 2:2, 4)
2. the company of the prophets from the city (2 Kings 2:3, 5)
3. his cloak (2 Kings 2:8)
4. divided to the right and to the left (2 Kings 2:8)
5. horses of fire (2 Kings 2:11)

Day 7: Book of Romans

1. that we are God's children (Romans 8:16)
2. sufferings (Romans 8:17)
3. the creation (Romans 8:20)
4. childbirth (Romans 8:22)
5. the Spirit (Romans 8:26)